CURIOUS LISTS for Kids

HUMAN BODY

To my partner in life, Fer, who always turns on a light on the darkness. IM

For all those who help us to look after ourselves and stay healthy. RB

A Raspberry Book
www.raspberrybooks.co.uk
Written by Rachel Delahaye
Illustrated by Isabel Muñoz

Editorial: Tracey Turner and Kathryn Jewitt
Consultant: Dr. Patricia Macnair
Art direction: Sidonie Beresford-Browne
Design: Sidonie Beresford-Browne and Rachael Fisher

LONDON & NEW YORK

Text and design copyright © Raspberry Books Ltd 2020
First published 2020 in the United States by Kingfisher,
120 Broadway, New York, NY 10271
Kingfisher is an imprint of
Macmillan Children's Books, London
All rights reserved.

Distributed in the U.S. and Canada by Macmillan,
120 Broadway, New York, NY 10271

Library of Congress Cataloging-in-Publication Data has been applied for.

ISBN 978-0-7534-7655-0

Kingfisher books are available for special promotions and premiums.
For details contact: Special Markets Department, Macmillan, 120 Broadway,
New York, NY 10271

For more information, please visit
www.kingfisherbooks.com

Printed in China
3 5 7 9 8 6 4 2
2TR/1020/WKT/RV/128MA

CURIOUS LISTS for Kids

HUMAN BODY

Rachel Delahaye ✳ Isabel Muñoz

KINGFISHER
LONDON & NEW YORK

10 ASTONISHING FACTS *About* HUMANS

Other animals outnumber us and many are much stronger, but human beings rule the planet—at least for the time being. We've covered 40 percent of the Earth's land surface in crops and grazing, built more than 75,000 towns and cities, and traveled into space. And what goes on inside our bodies is even more astonishing . . .

1. Laid end to end, the arteries, veins, and capillaries in the adult human body would stretch 100,000 miles (160,000 km), which is four times around the Earth.

2. The human body is made up of around 100 trillion cells.

3. Those cells contain around 7 octillion atoms. Written out, that's 7,000,000,000,000,000,000,000,000,000.

4. We can see around 1 million colors and detect a trillion different smells.

5. In a single day our blood travels 11,800 miles (19,000 km) as it circulates around the body.

6. There are more bacteria in one human mouth than there are people in the whole world.

7. The brain contains 86 billion nerve cells joined by 100 trillion connections—that's more than the number of stars in the Milky Way.

8. We can recognize a sound in around 0.05 seconds—ten times faster than the blink of an eye.

9. The human body contains enough carbon to make 900 pencils.

10. Human bones are five times stronger than steel.

5 Foods That Make *You* FART

When you eat, food is broken down and the nutrients are absorbed into the body. This process produces gases, which need to find a way out of the body, either as burps or farts. These foods are common gas-producers:

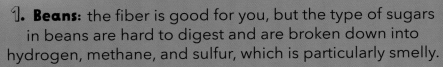

1. **Beans:** the fiber is good for you, but the type of sugars in beans are hard to digest and are broken down into hydrogen, methane, and sulfur, which is particularly smelly.

2. **The onion family:** onions, garlic, and leeks contain sugars called fructans that create gas.

3. **High-fiber vegetables:** high-fiber green vegetables are good for us, but can be hard to digest. When something is not quickly broken down by our stomach acid, the bacteria in the guts get to work on it, which creates gas . . . **with a smell**.

4. **Dairy products:** dairy products contain a sugar called lactose which is broken down in the gut by an enzyme called lactase. Around 65 percent of adults have low levels of lactase and can't break lactose down. Instead it passes through the gut to the large bowel where bacteria ferment it, releasing gas.

5. **Fatty meats:** fatty foods slow down digestion, but fatty meats also contain an acid called methionine. Bacteria breaks the methionine down into **stinky** hydrogen sulfide.

6 HEAVIEST INTERNAL ORGANS

The skin is by far the biggest and heaviest of the body's organs, with an average weight of 9.9 pounds (4.5 kg). One of its jobs is to keep the following internal organs inside us!

1. **Liver** 3.44 pounds (1.56 kg)
2. Brain **3 pounds (1.4 kg)**
3. **Lungs** 2.87 pounds (1.3 kg)
4. Heart **0.66 pound (0.3 kg)**
5. **Kidneys** 0.57 pound (0.26 kg)
6. Spleen **0.386 pound (0.175 kg)**

9 PAIRS OF BODY PARTS

Despite all these things coming in twos, humans can manage with just one of each.

1. Ears
2. Eyes
3. Hands
4. Feet
5. Arms
6. Legs
7. Nipples
8. Kidneys
9. Lungs

5 Famous People *with* Extra Fingers *and* Toes

Having an extra finger or toe is called polydactyly and affects about one in a thousand people. It often runs in families. The ancient people of Chaco Canyon, New Mexico, celebrated polydactyly and even decorated their houses with six-toed footprints. Here are some famous polydactyl people.

1.
Anne Boleyn
The second wife of King Henry VIII was said to have had six fingers on her right hand (later she was short of one head).

2.
Henry II The Pious
Henry was High Duke of all Poland from 1238 to 1241, and had six toes on his left foot.

3.
Gemma Arterton
The British actress and James Bond star was born with an extra finger on each hand. They contained no bones and were removed at birth.

4.
Robert Chambers
Chambers was a 19th-century geologist, writer, scientist, and thinker. He had six fingers on each hand and six toes on both feet.

5.
Theodore Roosevelt
"Hound Dog" **Taylor**
The American blues musician was born with six fingers on his left hand, which perhaps explains why he was so good at blues guitar.

5 SPEEDY REACTIONS

1. Some pain signals **can travel at up to 268 mph (431 km/h).**
2. The fastest **nerve impulses** travel at a speed of 267 mph (430 km/h).
3. **The burst of air from** a cough can be as fast as 59 mph (95 km/h).
4. **A sneeze** explodes at around 8.9 mph (14.4 km/h).
5. **The** blink of an eye **takes a tenth of a second.**

5 *Flowers* That Are BAD For You

We tend to think of flowers as pretty and harmless, but these ones grow in abundance in woodlands and aren't so friendly. If eaten they can cause dizziness, stomach pains, and even death.

1. **Deadly nightshade** *(Atropa belladonna)*
2. **Foxglove** *(Digitalis purpurea)*
3. **Lords-and-ladies** *(Arum maculatum)*
4. **Monkshood** *(Aconitum napellus)*
5. **Poison hemlock** *(Conium maculatum)*

5 *Flowers* That Are GOOD For You

Of course, some flowers are as kind as they are pretty. These are easy to spot, and can do you the world of good—but NEVER pick and eat anything unless you have an expert with you.

1. **Dandelion:** both flowers and leaves (cleaned) can be eaten and are full of nutrients.
2. **Marigold:** flowers help to reduce swelling and can be rubbed onto bites and stings to soothe.
3. **Nasturtium:** a colorful decoration for salads that also fights infection.
4. **Lavender:** widely used to aid restful sleep and reduce stress.
5. **Evening primrose:** oil extracted from the leaves contains phenylalanine, which is a pain reliever.

5 Things About WASP STINGS

We're scared of big animals like lions and sharks, but little ones are more often a pain.

1. Wasps have a sting that injects chemicals that trigger pain receptors and break down cells.

2. Wasp stings can cause swelling and itching, wheezing or gasping, dizziness and vomiting.

3. The effects of a sting usually wear off in about 24 hours.

4. When a wasp stings, it releases chemicals that make other wasps nearby become more aggressive.

5. For a very small minority of people, a wasp sting can cause a severe allergic reaction, which can be deadly.

5 Common Allergies

Allergies aren't the fault of the thing we're allergic to—it's the immune system treating it as dangerous. In an allergic reaction all sorts of chemicals, including one called histamine, flood the body and cause things like itching, sneezing, and wheezing. In severe cases the blood pressure can drop very low, and the airways block off. This is known as anaphylactic shock and it can be fatal. We can over-react to lots of things:

1. An allergy to pollen is known as hay fever. Spring and summer can be uncomfortable seasons for sufferers.

2. Pet dandruff—called dander—can be an allergen. It contains skin, saliva, and particles of dirt and pollen. Try not to think about that too much next time you pat a dog.

3. People can be allergic to different medicines. The most common medicine allergen is an antibiotic called penicillin.

4. The most common food allergens are nuts, eggs, cow's milk, and shellfish.

5. People can be allergic to wasp and bee stings, which can be very dangerous.

10 Brainy Bits

ONE brain

TWO hemispheres—the two sides of the cerebrum, separated by a groove.

THREE sections—the cerebrum, cerebellum, and brain stem.

FOUR lobes—areas of the brain responsible for different skills.

1. **Hypothalamus:** transmits information affecting hormones, controls temperature

2. **Thalamus:** relay station for sensory and motor information, and regulates sleep

3. **Hippocampus:** forms new memories, involved in learning

4. **Corpus callosum:** passes information between the two hemispheres of the cerebrum

5. **Pituitary gland:** secretes hormones into bloodstream

6. **Midbrain:** eye movement, sight, and hearing

7. **Pons:** involved in breathing, communication between different parts of the brain, and the senses

8. **Medulla oblongata:** regulates breathing and blood circulation

9. **Cerebellum:** movement, co-ordination, and balance

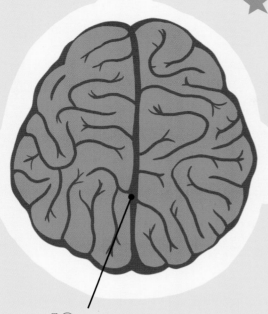

10. Cerebral cortex: cerebrum's outer layer. Many jobs including emotional expression, vision, language and sensory processing, and motor functions.

3 FAMOUS Brains

1. Albert Einstein
was a brilliant scientist. After he died in 1955, his brain was carved into slices, some of which can be seen in the Mütter Museum in Philadelphia and The National Museum of Health and Medicine in Maryland, both in the USA.

2. Charles Babbage
was an inventor and mathematician who created the first example of an automatic calculator. When he died in 1887 his brain was divided, and is now kept in the Hunterian Museum and the Science Museum, both in London, UK.

3. Vladimir Lenin
was a Russian revolutionary and leader of Soviet Russia and the Soviet Union. After he died in 1925, his brain was sliced up and studied. It's been preserved and is kept in the Moscow Institute of Brain Research, Russia.

8 Rare and Remarkable BRAIN Disorders

Brains are like finely tuned computers, so a brain injury or brain surgery can have some very peculiar side effects. These are fascinating and very rare.

1. Gourmand syndrome
The patient becomes obsessed with gourmet food.

2. Alien hand syndrome
One hand moves things all on its own, as if the owner can't control it.

3. Foreign accent syndrome
Speaking uncontrollably in a foreign accent, or perhaps more than one.

4. Hemispatial neglect
Ignoring or unable to see half the world. Sufferers may only eat food from one side of their plate, draw only half an object, or see only one side of a clock.

5. Prosopagnia or face blindness
Difficulty in recognizing faces, even familiar ones, and sometimes even their own!

6. Mirror-touch syndrome
Feeling what is being experienced by others. A sufferer will feel hugged if they see another person being hugged, or feel that their mouth is full if they watch someone eating.

7. Capgra syndrome
Believing that loved ones have been replaced by strangers, imposters, robots, or aliens!

8. Cotard's delusion
Believing oneself to be dead. Sufferers may refuse to eat and choose to hang out in cemeteries, thinking it's where they belong.

5 Historical CURES for BALDNESS

1. Rub myrrh berries into the scalp—Ancient Roman cure

2. Burn bees, then rub the ash onto the scalp—Saxon cure

3. Mix fat from a hippo, a crocodile, a cat, a snake, and an ibex, then rub the mixture onto the scalp—Ancient Egyptian cure

4. Rub cold tea and slices of lemon into the scalp—Victorian cure

5. Apply a mixture of horseradish, beetroot, spices, and pigeon droppings—Ancient Greek cure

5 Great APES

Human beings are great apes. We share more than 95 percent of our genetic make-up with chimpanzees. We are the only great ape that isn't endangered.

1. Bonobo (once known as a pygmy chimpanzee)

2. Chimpanzee

3. Gorilla

4. Orangutan

5. Modern human

6 Facts About Kissing

1. When two people kiss, they exchange between 10 million and 1 billion bacteria.

2. Adrenaline is released during a kiss, which can make your heart beat faster.

3. Kissing releases dopamine, a brain chemical associated with good feelings.

4. Kissing shuts down negative emotions and reactions, such as tension.

5. Kissing can use around 24 facial muscles, and burns around two calories a minute!

6. The science of kissing is called philematology.

5 WAYS Technology Is Affecting Our HEALTH

Computers are useful and keep us connected and entertained, but there are some downsides to having the world at your fingertips all day, every day…

1. **We blink less when staring at a screen, which makes eyes dry and sore.**

2. We're becoming more easily distracted and less able to retain information.

3. **Taking selfies can make people more self-obsessed.**

4. Comparing ourselves with others online can cause low self-esteem.

5. **Spending too long online and gaming means we spend more time sitting down, and might not get enough exercise.**

6 MEDICAL WORDS for Everyday Things

1. **Horripilation:** goosebumps

2. **The cutaneous system:** skin

3. **Dermatoglyphics:** fingerprints

4. **Pruritus:** itching

5. **Borborygmus:** rumbling stomach

6. **Epistaxis:** nosebleed

4 Food TATTOOS

Some people love their food so much that they've ordered their favorite meal as body art in permanent ink.

1. A man from England has a full English breakfast tattooed on the top of his head. The breakfast includes bacon, eggs, sausages, and beans, complete with a plate and cutlery.

2. **A slice of ham and pineapple pizza appears across the back of the head of a man from Wales.**

3. Grilled cheese sandwiches, burgers, and hot dogs are popular, and appear on people's arms, legs, and other body parts all over the world.

4. **Dim sum and ramen are also worldwide favorites—an American man has a tattoo of a square of uncooked instant ramen on his arm to celebrate his favorite nighttime snack.**

6 Curious Body Bits and Pieces

1. Appendix
A finger-like tube on the large intestine. It is home to bacteria that help the gut.

2. Dimples
Indents on either side of the mouth which show up when we smile. Some think they are caused by shorter facial muscles. Others think that it's where the largest facial muscle has formed in two parts instead of one.

3. Belly button
A knob in the middle of the tummy where the umbilical cord (which joined you to your mother before you were born) was once attached. The cord is cut or falls off shortly after birth and seals itself. Some people have an outy "knot," but most have an inny—a small dip.

4. Adam's apple
A lump of stretchy tissue called cartilage at the front of the larynx, halfway down the neck. It strengthens the throat, protects the vocal cords, and is more noticeable in men than women.

5. Wisdom teeth
A big set of molar teeth at the back of the mouth which usually come through from later teens onward. They once helped our ancient ancestors to grind tough food!

6. Uvula
A dangly pendulum in the back of the throat that secretes saliva.

5 FART Gases

1.
Nitrogen, which makes up most of the air we breathe.

2.
Oxygen, also found in the air.

3.
Carbon dioxide, the same gas you breathe out.

4.
Hydogen, which can mix with sulfur to make hydrogen sulfide, a very smelly gas.

5.
Methane, which is flammable.

5 Facts About PAIN

Pain is horrible, so why do we have it and how is it made?

1. We feel pain when nerve receptors under the skin send signals through the spinal cord to our brain.

2. Pain tells us that we need to take extra care, and warns us when we are sick or damaging our bodies.

3. Anesthesia is the word for a chemical or method that numbs pain. It is given to a patient during an operation that would be extremely painful otherwise.

4. The brain doesn't have any pain receptors. Brain surgeons can operate without the patient needing an anesthetic.

5. Congenital analgesia is an extremely rare condition where a person cannot feel physical pain. Although not feeling pain sounds like a good thing, it's an extremely dangerous condition to have—if you don't feel pain, you don't know when something is too hot and burning you, for example.

6 Peculiar Marathons

1. Space Run: in 2016 British astronaut Tim Peake ran a marathon on his treadmill in space, coinciding with the London Marathon back on Earth.

2. Man Versus Horse: this marathon with a difference takes place in Llanwrtyd Wells, Wales. The winner is usually a horse.

3. Midnight Sun Marathon: in Tromsø in Norway, the sun doesn't set in summer. This is an evening marathon run on June 22 every year, and contestants must finish by midnight.

4. The North Pole Marathon: not for the faint-hearted—running across sea ice in freezing temperatures, often meeting polar bears on the way.

5. The Antarctic Ice Marathon: takes place in November, when temperatures can drop as low as -4 °F (-20 °C).

6. The Marathon de Medoc: this French event requires participants to stop as many times as they can along the course to drink wine and eat French delicacies.

HOW
Digestion Works in 6 Easy Steps

1 Chewing mashes food into easy-to-swallow chunks. The saliva in the mouth contains enzymes that start chemical reactions to break down the food.

2 Swallowed food travels down to the stomach inside a tube called the esophagus. The muscles in the tube contract to squeeze the food down. This is called *peristalsis*.

3 The stomach releases juices made up of fat-busting bile, sent to the stomach by the liver, and hydrochloric acid, which attacks harmful bacteria and also breaks down proteins.

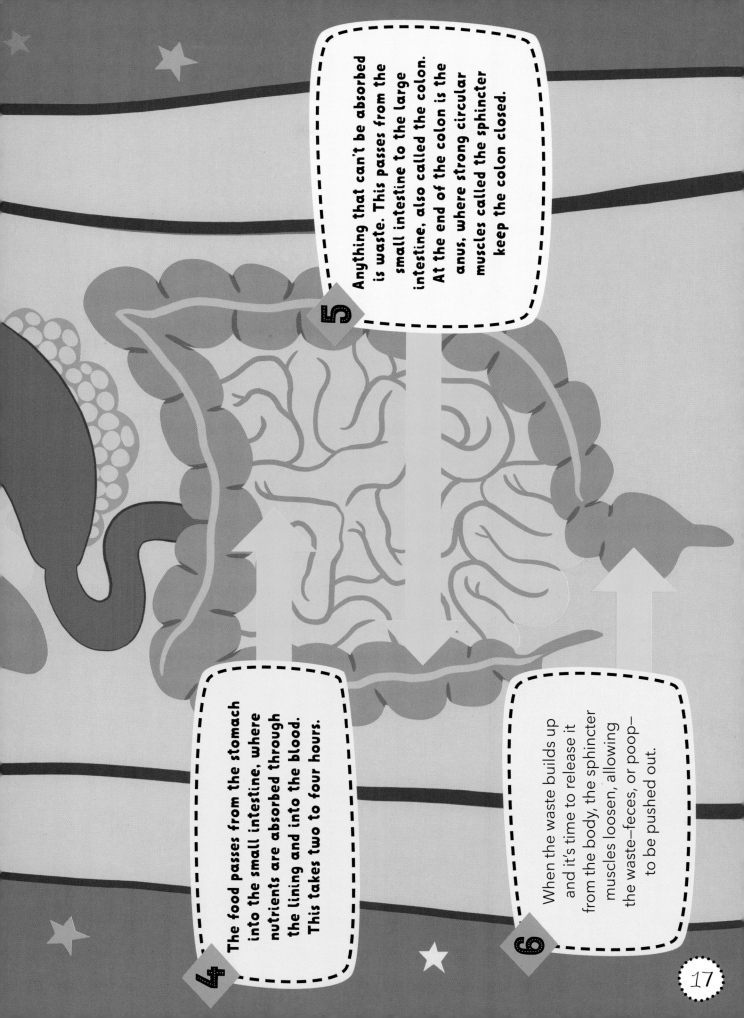

5

Anything that can't be absorbed is waste. This passes from the small intestine to the large intestine, also called the colon. At the end of the colon is the anus, where strong circular muscles called the sphincter keep the colon closed.

4

The food passes from the stomach into the small intestine, where nutrients are absorbed through the lining and into the blood. This takes two to four hours.

6

When the waste builds up and it's time to release it from the body, the sphincter muscles loosen, allowing the waste—feces, or poop— to be pushed out.

9 Facts About Feet

....

1. Each foot contains 26 bones—one quarter of all the bones in your body are in your feet!

2. Feet have 250,000 sweat glands and can produce 8.5 ounces (1/4 liter) of sweat per day.

3. There are around 200,000 nerve endings in our feet, which is why they are so ticklish.

4. Feet work best when bare. Shoes can prevent the "rolling" movement from heel to toe which spreads our weight evenly.

5. When the toe closest to the big toe is longer than the big toe, it's called "Morton's toe."

6. The Achilles tendon attaches the heel bone to the calf muscle. It's the strongest tendon in the body, but can suddenly snap!

7. Well-controlled toes can do incredible things, such as writing, painting, and archery.

8. Smelly feet can actually be cheesy! It is possible to make cheese from the bacteria that feed on foot sweat. Would you want to, though?

9. Each foot takes 1.5 times your body weight when you walk. When running, each foot takes up to 5 times your body weight.

13 Body Part Transplants

All of these body parts can be transplanted from one human to another, improving or saving the life of the person who receives them.

1. Heart
2. Liver
3. Kidneys
4. Lungs
5. Pancreas
6. Small intestines
7. Corneas (part of the eyes)
8. Skin
9. Veins and arteries
10. Heart valves
11. Tendons
12. Ligaments
13. Bones

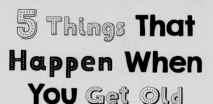

5 Things **That Happen When YOU** Get Old

1. **Skin loses elasticity and gets thinner, causing wrinkles.**

2. Bones can become weaker and more likely to fracture or break.

3. **Bones in the spine can compact, making people up to 2 inches (5 cm) shorter!**

4. Changes in the inner ear can damage or kill the tiny hairs that translate sound waves into sound.

5. **Some parts of the brain shrink as you age and communication between the nerve cells becomes slower, affecting memory.**

5 SMALL Ways to BURN More CALORIES

1. Fidget while you watch TV! You can burn five times more calories than sitting still.

2. Take the stairs—you'll burn way more than standing in an elevator.

3. Household chores are workouts! Cleaning the bath for 15 minutes can burn 100 calories.

4. Laughing can make the metabolism up to 20 percent faster, burning more calories.

5. Take a layer off—being cool makes your body burn energy to get warm.

7 Gruesome Worms

There are worms that can live inside the human body. Most of them get there when people unknowingly eat the worms' eggs, either in uncooked food or by touching a contaminated surface and then touching the mouth.

1. **Roundworms** hatch and live in the intestines. They can grow up to 14 inches (35 cm) long, and cause tummy upsets.

2. **Tapeworms** attach to the wall of the intestines and eat digested food, causing all sorts of nasty symptoms.

3. **Threadworms** live in the gut and then wriggle down to the anus to lay their eggs, which causes severe bottom itching.

4. **Loa loa** are worms transmitted by a deerfly bite. They sometimes live in the eye, causing pain and even blindness.

5. **Whipworms** live in the gut, causing upset stomachs.

7 Reasons Why We Dream

No one can absolutely explain why we build pictures and stories in our minds while we sleep, but here are some theories:

1. The things we long for in life play out in our minds but sometimes get jumbled up.

2. Our brain tries to make pictures of all the signals and information produced by our bodies during sleep.

3. We are sorting out all the new information we have learned during the day.

5. Our brains are going through new and old memories.

4. Dreams prepare us for new experiences or future threats.

6. Dreams teach us how to retain information.

7. Our dreams help us come to terms with problems.

5 Tell-Tale Nail Signs

In healthy nails the area attached to the skin should be pink. Anything else may be a sign that a check-up is needed.

1. **Pale** nails can be a sign of an unhealthy diet.

2. **Yellow** nails may mean there's a fungal infection.

3. Nails that have **ridges and pits** can be a sign of a skin condition.

4. If nails are **blue** it can indicate a lack of oxygen.

5. Nails that **crack and split** easily could mean there's a problem with the thyroid gland.

7 FACTS About Nails

1. Fingernails grow around 0.14 inch (3.5 mm) per month.

2. Fingernails grow much faster than toenails.

3. Nails are made out of a protein called keratin.

4. The cuticle is the seal between nail and finger, and keeps germs out of the skin.

5. Humans and other primates (apes, monkeys, and other monkey-like creatures) have nails. Other mammals have claws.

6. Nails on your dominant hand grow faster—so if you're right-handed, the nails on your right hand grow faster.

7. Nails grow more quickly in the summer.

3 Record-breaking DIVERS

1.

Free diver

The current world record holder for diving with no breathing apparatus is Austrian Herbert Nitsch—702 feet (214 m).

2.

Scuba diver

Ahmed Gabr set the world record for the deepest scuba dive—1,090.39 feet (332.35 m).

3.

Deep-sea submarine explorer

Victor Vescovo is the current record holder—35,850 feet (10,927 m). In April 2019, he descended in a deep-sea submersible to the deepest known place in the world—the Pacific Ocean's Mariana Trench.

4 Effects of Deep-sea Diving on the Body

The deeper you dive, the more water there is pushing against your body. As water pressure increases, the volume of air in your body decreases. This can cause problems as you go down and come back up again.

1. Pain in the sinuses, which are between your eyes.

2. Pain in the ears.

3. Coming up, the pressure decreases and the air in your lungs expands, making it harder to breathe.

4. If you dive to 100 feet (30 m) or more and rise up to the surface too quickly, you can get decompression sickness, also known as the bends. It can be very serious and sometimes deadly.

8 Facts About the Human Voice

Here are some facts about the human voice to get you talking:

1. Your voice box, or larynx, is the reason you are able to speak, sing, laugh, hum, whisper, and make any number of weird noises. Everyone's voice is unique!

2. The voice box is a small tube at the top of your windpipe, which contains folds of tissue called vocal cords that expand and contract. When air rushes over the cords it causes them to vibrate, producing sound. Movements of the mouth, jaw, lips, and tongue shape the words.

3. Muscles lengthen and tense the vocal cords to control sound production. The tighter your vocal cords, the higher the sound produced.

4. At around the age of 13, a boy's vocal cords grow longer, making his voice get deeper.

5. Opera singers and pop stars train their vocal cords to make their voice more powerful, just like athletes train their muscles.

6. Some languages use sounds that are not made by the vocal cords—some African languages have a "click" noise made by just the tongue.

7. Your vocal cords stop food, drink, and saliva from entering your windpipe and choking you.

8. If your vocal cords become inflamed or infected, they can swell up so you lose your voice.

7 AGES OF MAN

In his comedy play, *As You Like It*, William Shakespeare describes seven different stages of life.

1. Birth and infancy

2. SCHOOLCHILD

3. Teenager

7 Questions About the Human Body That have NO ANSWERS... YET

There are theories, but no proper answers for any of these.

1. Why do we yawn?

2. Why do we have different blood types?

3. Why are our ape relatives—gorillas, chimps, and orangutans—so much stronger than us?

4. Why is laughter catching?

5. Why do we experience déjà vu? (Déjà vu is French for "already seen.") It refers to the feeling of already having experienced something exactly the same as whatever is happening now.

6. Why do we have a dominant hand?

7. Why do we dream?

4. Young adult

5. Middle-aged adult

6. Old age

7. VERY OLD AGE AND DEATH

3 of the WORLD'S Fastest Ever Sprinters

The 100 m sprint is an athletics event that reveals just how fast the human body can go. So far, these sprinters are the fastest of all time.

1. Usain Bolt
from Jamaica, 9.58 seconds

2. Tyson Gay
from USA, 9.69 seconds

3. Yohan Blake
from Jamaica, 9.69 seconds

6 HUMAN Body Museums

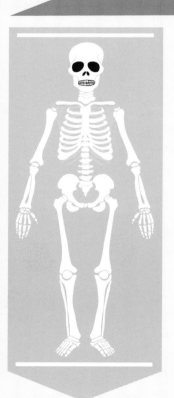

1. The Corpus Museum is an interactive museum in Oegstgeest, Netherlands, where you can walk through giant models of parts of the body.

2. The Human Body Museum in Bangkok, Thailand, has 14 dissected human bodies to view.

3. Body Worlds is a traveling exhibition that visits museums all over the world. It has many human specimens and reconstructions of human poses using real body parts.

4. The Mütter Museum in Philadelphia has a large collection of human and medical specimens.

5. The Science Museum in London has over 1,000 human remains, including skeletons, mummies, and human tissue.

6. The Anatomical Museum in Athens, Greece, has human hands and hearts, and even faces!

5 BODY PARTS Used for FORTUNE-TELLING

There is absolutely no proof that any kind of fortune-telling works, but some people are convinced that different parts of the body can predict what's around the corner!

1. NAEVIOLOGY: marks on the body such as moles and birthmarks.

2. GASTROMANCY: sounds made in the stomach.

3. METOPOSCOPY: face shape and details.

4. CHIROMANCY: shape of the hands and lines on the palm.

5. PHRENOLOGY: size and shape of the skull.

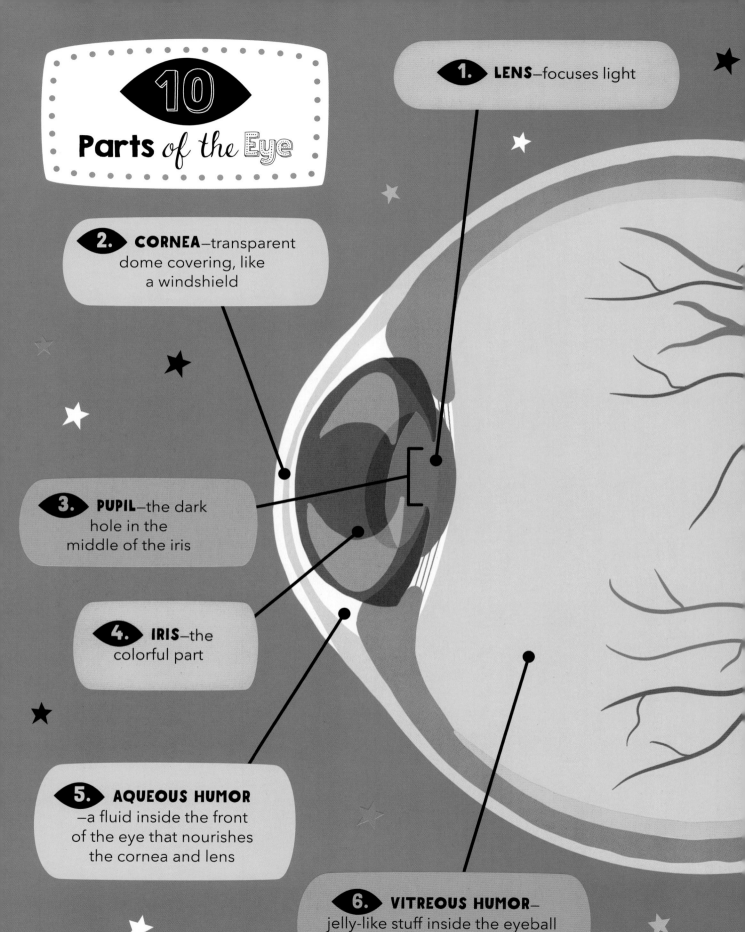

10
Parts of the Eye

1. **LENS**—focuses light

2. **CORNEA**—transparent dome covering, like a windshield

3. **PUPIL**—the dark hole in the middle of the iris

4. **IRIS**—the colorful part

5. **AQUEOUS HUMOR**—a fluid inside the front of the eye that nourishes the cornea and lens

6. **VITREOUS HUMOR**—jelly-like stuff inside the eyeball that keeps the eye's shape

7. **RETINA**—changes the light into nerve signals

8. **SCLERA**—the white of the eye, a protective coat

9. **OPTIC NERVE**—carries the messages to the brain

10. **MACULA**—contains sensory cells and determines how accurate your vision is

How the EYE Works *in* 5 STEPS

You actually see with your brain, not your eyes. The eye works like a camera, capturing light and sending data back to the brain.

1.
Light travels through the cornea to the iris.

2.
The iris protects the eye by controlling how much light is allowed in through the pupil, using muscles around it to relax and contract.

3.
The light enters the pupil and hits the lens, focusing the light onto the retina at the back of the eye.

4.
When light hits the retina it is turned upside down because the cornea is curved. It's like the reflection in a drop of water.

5.
The optic nerve attached to the retina carries all the details about the light— its shape and color—to the brain, which allows us to see an image.

5 PRESERVED Body Parts of Famous People

1. **Che Guevara**—Argentinian revolutionary: hair
2. **Buddha**—Indian spiritual leader: tooth
3. **Galileo Galilei**—Italian mathematician and astronomer: middle finger
4. **Abraham Lincoln**—American president: skull pieces
5. **Benito Mussolini**—Italian dictator: bits of brain

7 Ways to Detect Stress

Stress is what you feel when you are worried or uncomfortable about something. As well as changing the way you feel it can affect you physically too. Here are seven symptoms:

1. **Low energy**
2. **Headaches**
3. **Upset stomach, including diarrhea, constipation, and nausea**
4. **Aches, pains, and tense muscles**
5. **Chest pain and rapid heartbeat**
6. **Not being able to sleep**
7. **Frequent colds and infections**

4 FANCY Names for Human Habits

1. **Bruxism**—grinding your teeth
2. **Onychophagia**—biting your nails
3. **Trichophagia**—chewing your hair
4. **Rhinotillexomania**—picking your nose

3 Ways to Combat Stress

Too much stress is bad for our health. Knowing how to de-stress is important.

1. **Get plenty of regular exercise.**
2. **Take time to do relaxing things.**
3. **Laughter is a great stress-buster, so see or do something funny and have a good laugh.**
4. **Try meditating, or another relaxation technique.**
5. **Make sure you get plenty of sleep.**

8 Reasons to Meditate

Meditation is a state of being still, both in the body and in the mind. It has been practiced all over the world for thousands of years and has been proved to have many health benefits, including these:

1. **Reducing stress**
2. **Lowering blood pressure**
3. **Making you more patient**
4. **Boosting the immune system**
5. **Improving concentration and focus**
6. **Helping to keep the brain nimble as it gets older**
7. **Improving self-awareness**
8. **Controlling pain**

HOW TO MEDITATE
in 7 Steps

Meditation takes practice, but you have to start somewhere!

1. Find a comfortable sitting or lying position and close your eyes.

2. **Take slow, deep breaths.**

3. Focus on your muscles relaxing in every part of your body.

4. **Now breathe calmly and naturally.**

5. Pay attention to the feeling of the air passing in and out of your body.

6. **Let thoughts come in and out of your head—don't dwell on them.**

7. Do this for one minute. Try to build it up over time.

11 Firsts in TRANSPLANT History

Transplants can save lives, but they can be extremely difficult. That's why the first successful transplant operations are remembered and celebrated.

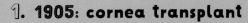

1. **1905: cornea transplant**
2. 1950: **kidney transplant**
3. 1966: **pancreas transplant**
4. 1967: **liver transplant**
5. **1967: heart transplant**
6. 1986: **double-lung transplant**
7. 1998: **hand transplant**
8. 2005: **partial face transplant**
9. **2008: complete full double arm**
10. 2010: **full facial transplant**
11. 2011: **double leg transplant**

4 Healthy Diets

1. Mediterranean diet
Full of fruit, vegetables, whole grains, beans, olive oil, fish, and small amounts of meat.

2. Traditional Japanese Okinawa diet
Plenty of fruit and vegetables with small amounts of fish and lean meat.

3. Nordic
Lots of vegetables, whole grain bread, oily fish, small amounts of low-fat fermented milk and cheese, and very small amounts of red meat.

4. West African
Whole grains, beans, starchy carbohydrates, vegetables, lean meat, and fish, full of fiber and essential good fats.

6 ANIMALS MEASURED in Humans

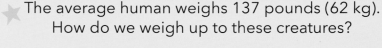

The average human weighs 137 pounds (62 kg). How do we weigh up to these creatures?

1. **BLUE WHALE**–about 380,000 pounds (173,000 kg) = **around 2,800 humans**
2. **AFRICAN ELEPHANT**–14,000 pounds (6,350 kg) = **102 humans**
3. **RHINO**–5,070 pounds (2,300 kg) = **37 humans**
4. **BROWN BEAR**–2,000 pounds (907 kg) = **14.5 humans**
5. **SALTWATER CROCODILE**–1,000 pounds (453 kg) = **7 humans**
6. **SIBERIAN TIGER**–770 pounds (350 kg) = **5.5 humans**

9 Remarkable FACTS About the LIVER

The liver is a super-important organ. Here's why:

1. The liver weighs about 2.9 pounds (1.3 kg)—about as much as a big hardback book.

2. **It's the biggest internal organ, and the second biggest organ in the body after the skin.**

3. It cleans the blood and cleans toxins out of the body.

4. **It processes the nutrients that the body needs.**

5. It produces bile, which breaks down fats in the digestive system.

6. **It makes good cholesterol, which helps to destroy bad fats.**

7. It plays an important role in helping the body to fight illness.

8. **It makes and stores energy for when the body needs a burst of it.**

9. It can regenerate, even if only a quarter of it is left.

3 FACTS About Snoring

1. Snoring can be hereditary: nearly 70 percent of snorers have snoring relatives.

2. Snoring can be as loud as 100 decibels, which is the same as a pneumatic drill.

3. The snoring sound is caused by air vibrating the breathing cavities in the head.

4 Reasons to Get a GOOD NIGHT'S Sleep

1. **Good sleep helps concentration and learning. Not having enough sleep can make newly learned information more difficult to store in the brain.**

2. Getting enough sleep can help you feel happier.

3. **Lack of sleep can make you eat more calories than you need.**

4. Good sleep helps you fight off illness.

4 Toilet-themed Places to Visit

1. Sulabh Museum of Toilets, New Delhi, India

2. Toilet History Museum, Kyiv, Ukraine

3. Toilet Seat Art Museum, Texas, USA

4. Toilet Culture Museum, Suwon, South Korea

4 Hominins That Have Died Out

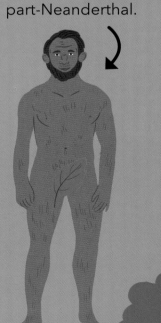

Modern human beings, or **Homo sapiens**, are the only human species that's still around. Here are some of our close relatives, called hominins, from long ago. This is a just small selection—more than 20 hominins have been discovered so far.

1. Homo habilis was a human-like species that used tools and first appeared about 2 million years ago.

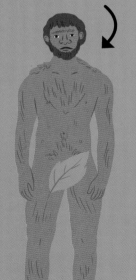

2. Homo erectus lived from about 2 million years ago to about 200,000 years ago, and perhaps even more recently than that.

3. Homo Heidelbergensis lived from about 600,000 to 250,000 years ago. It's thought that they were the first hominins to build shelters.

4. Homo Neanderthalis lived at the same time as Homo sapiens. Our species and Neanderthals lived and had babies together. Many of us are part-Neanderthal.

11 Facts About Hair

1. On average there are 100,000–150,000 hairs in a full head of hair.

2. Hair can stretch up to 30 percent longer when wet.

3. Hair is made out of keratin, the same stuff as nails.

4. While 90 percent of your hair is growing, 10 percent is "resting" —a short period of doing nothing before it drops out.

5. Hair grows around 6 inches (15 cm) a year.

6. If you pluck out a hair a new one starts growing immediately.

7. Scientists can tell how healthy a person's diet is by looking at the protein levels in their hair.

8. Hair covers the entire body apart from palms, soles, and lips.

9. Humans have the same number of hair follicles per square inch as chimpanzees.

10. Intelligent people have more zinc and copper in their hair, but scientists still don't know why!

11. Less than 4 percent of the world are natural redheads.

7 Ideals of Female Beauty Through the Ages

What is thought to be beautiful changes according to when and where you are in the world.

1. Ancient Egypt—slender body, symmetrical face, lots of make up, and braided wigs.

2. Ancient Greece—pale skin with one long brow (unibrow), bleached curly hair, plump body.

3. Han Dynasty, China—small feet, narrow waist, pale skin.

4. Heian Era, Japan—very long hair, smudged eyebrows, white face.

5. Renaissance Italy—curvy figure, fair skin, high forehead, light-colored hair.

6. 18th-century France—pale skin, plump face, and double chin.

7. 1920s Western countries—flat chest, slender figure, bobbed hair.

13 Things in Your Skin

Our skin is in three layers: the epidermis at the top, the dermis in the middle, and the hypodermis at the bottom. But there's a lot going on in between.

1 Hair shaft

2 **Epidermis**—creates a barrier and also contains the cells that give your skin its color

3 **Sebaceous gland**—releases oily sebum, which makes skin waterproof

4 **Hair follicle**—the root of the hair

5 **Sensory nerve endings**—react to outside stimuli such as temperature and touch

6 **Adipose tissue**—fatty layers which keep you warm and contain nutrients for the skin

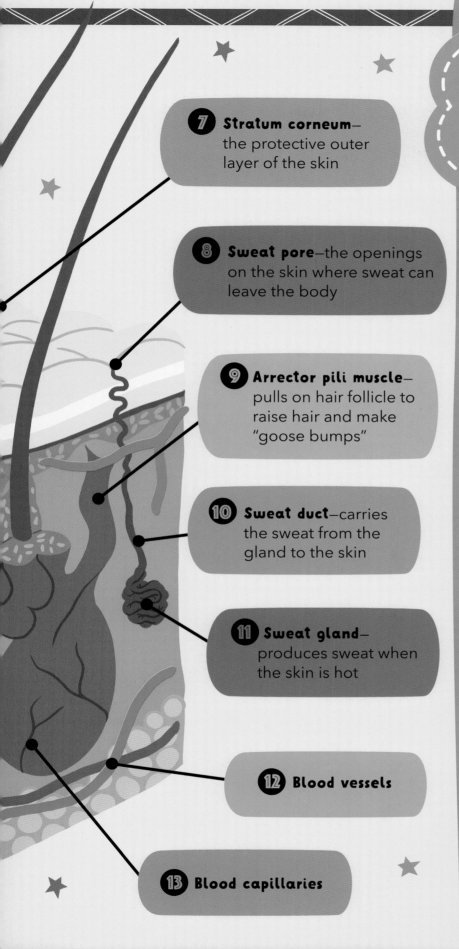

7 **Stratum corneum**— the protective outer layer of the skin

8 **Sweat pore**—the openings on the skin where sweat can leave the body

9 **Arrector pili muscle**— pulls on hair follicle to raise hair and make "goose bumps"

10 **Sweat duct**—carries the sweat from the gland to the skin

11 **Sweat gland**— produces sweat when the skin is hot

12 **Blood vessels**

13 **Blood capillaries**

10 Facts About SKIN

1. Skin is the largest organ in the human body.

2. It grows faster than any other part of the body.

3. Every hour you lose around 600,000 dead skin cells.

4. Skin renews itself every 28 days.

5. Skin is thickest on the soles of the feet.

6. Skin is very good at repairing itself if it's cut or grazed.

7. It detects changes in temperature so our bodies can respond.

8. Around 1,000 species of bacteria live on our skin.

9. There are types of fungi that live on the skin between our toes.

10. A replacement for skin has been developed, using cow tendons and silicon.

8 Reasons to Laugh

There is a saying, "Laughter is the best medicine," and there is no doubt that it does have health benefits! Laughing . . .

1. . . . makes you happy.

2. . . . lowers blood pressure.

3. . . . reduces stress.

4. . . . exercises your stomach muscles.

5. . . . boosts immunity.

6. . . . reduces pain.

7. . . . burns calories.

8. . . . helps you breathe better.

HA HA HA HA HA HA

3 Traditional Healers

1. Ngangkari, Western Desert, Central Australia
These Aboriginal healers listen to and watch the patient, and give massages and herbal remedies.

2. Babu, Tanzania
The Babu lives in a hut away from the community, and makes healing potions from local plants and herbs.

3. Curandero, Latin America and Mexico
The Curandero makes herbal potions and performs rituals involving essential oils, eggs, and prayer.

5 ORDINARY Foods to Be CAREFUL of

1. **Raw kidney beans** contain a toxic protein. They must be soaked and cooked before eating.

2. **Star fruit** is fine if you have healthy kidneys, but if not, the fruit's deadly toxin, caramboxin, can be very dangerous.

3. **Cassava** is a root vegetable that has to be cooked thoroughly, otherwise it can release the poison cyanide.

4. **Ackee** fruit must be ripe and prepared properly before eating. Unripe, it contains toxins that can kill.

5. **Rhubarb leaves** contain something called oxalic acid, which can make you very sick.

4 Funny Facial Treatments

These strange-sounding treatments for the face are supposed to make your skin look lovely. Tempted to give them a try?

1. **Bird poop facial**—made with the poop of a particular Japanese nightingale, it is supposed to heal scarring and give a deep clean.

2. **Caviar facial**—caviar is fish eggs, and it's meant to nourish your skin.

3. **Bee venom**—people use it because it's supposed to make skin look less wrinkly.

4. **Snail slime**—the slime is scooped up and smeared on—or why not let the snails roam over your face?

5 FACTS About Teeth

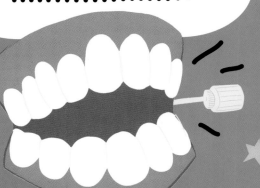

1. **Tooth enamel is the hardest part of your body.**

2. Teeth start to form even before you are born.

3. **Humans have two sets of teeth in their entire lifetime—baby teeth and permanent teeth.**

4. On average, a person spends 38.5 days brushing their teeth over their lifetime.

5. **One third of a tooth is underneath the gum line.**

SPOTS!

2. Pimples

Little bumps caused by oils or dirt trapped in the pores of the skin.

1. Boils

Large, pus-filled spots, infected by bacteria, which slide down the hair follicle into the skin.

3. Acne

Red spots on the shoulders, face, and neck, caused by oily secretions that block the tiny holes where hair comes out of the skin.

5. Whiteheads

Pores in the skin which have become clogged up with an oily white secretion called sebum.

4. Pustules

When pimples become infected they fill with pus, and become little blisters. So no squeezing those spots!

6. Blackheads

Blackheads are pores full of oily sebum which have turned black on the surface as they react with the air.

6 SKIN Disorders

1. PSORIASIS
Patches of itchy, overgrown scales of skin.

2. CELLULITIS
Swollen and red infected skin, tender and often hot to the touch.

3. ECZEMA
Extremely itchy patches of red or white inflamed skin that flake off.

4. CARBUNCLE
A hard, red swelling under the skin that may ooze pus.

5. ROSACEA
Usually on the face, skin is flushed red, tender, sometimes with bumps.

6. COLD SORE
A painful blister that appears on the edge of lips, caused by a virus.

The 5 Tastes

There are five recognized categories of flavor that our taste buds can detect.

1. **Sweet**—delicious sugary treats and fruits.

2. **Sour**—the taste that makes your lips curl. Think of lemons!

3. **Salty**—anything that has a sharp and salty taste.

4. **Bitter**—a taste that is both sharp and sour and sometimes unpleasant.

5. **Savoury**—also known as umami, this flavor is a blend of salty and sweet, like caramelized nuts or parmesan cheese.

6 Things We've Sniffed Out About NOSES

1. **The nose has 50 million special olfactory cells that help us to smell.**

2. Smelling is important for detecting dangerous chemicals or rotten food.

3. **Smelling is crucial in helping us to taste (try blocking your nose and eating!)**

4. The two nostrils are divided by a wall called the septum, which is made up of strong tissue called cartilage.

5. **When you breathe in through the nose, the nose cavity warms or cools the incoming air to body temperature.**

6. The nasal cavity is lined with little hairs to trap dust and particles.

10 EXTREME SPORTS

Some humans like to push themselves to the limits of their physical and mental capabilities. Here are some sports that need peak fitness and a big dose of bravery.

1

Wingsuit flying
Like BASE jumping (see right), except the jumper wears a special suit with built-in "wings." These create air pockets to give extra lift and control as the flyer glides through the air.

2

Ice climbing
Rock climbing—but up ice formations! It's a huge challenge to strength and endurance because of the cold weather and the slippy, sometimes unstable ice.

3

Paraskiing
A combination of snow skiing and parasailing (a cross between a parachute and a kite). The skier builds up speed, lifts up into the air, and then lands back on the skis.

4

Whitewater rafting
Navigating river rapids in an inflatable boat. Wear a helmet and hold on for dear life!

5 BASE jumping

Parachuting from a high platform, instead of a plane. BASE stands for Building, Antenna, Span, Earth.

6 Free solo climbing

Climbers scale sheer cliffs with no safety equipment whatsoever. Just strength, skill, and concentration. An extremely dangerous test of physical and mental strength.

7 Volcano surfing

Volcano surfers hike to the top of a volcano and slide down its gravelly side on a thin board. Of course, they only surf down volcanoes that aren't in danger of erupting, otherwise it really WOULD be an extreme (and definitely deadly) sport.

8 Downhill mountain biking

The spectacular racing sport of hurtling down super-steep, obstacle-covered slopes on a full-suspension mountain bike.

9 Parkour

Involves freestyle running, jumping, and climbing over, under, through, and around various obstacles. It's incredibly athletic, and often practiced in cityscapes.

10 Big-wave surfing

Surfers are towed out in boats to massive waves, usually at least 20 feet (6 m) high. This is super dangerous so it's for highly experienced surfers only.

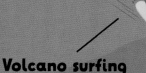

9 Signs of Good Health

You're more likely to be
in good health if you have:

1. Healthy teeth and gums
2. Strong nails
3. A healthy weight
4. Good sleep
5. Regular, healthy poop

6. A friendship circle or support network
7. A clean, pink tongue
8. A diet full of vegetables, protein, and good fats
9. An interest in your physical and emotional health

5 MUSCLE-POWERED Weightlifting Moves

Weightlifting involves lifting a bar that's loaded with weights. It requires great strength in the thigh and arm muscles, not to mention the core abdominal muscles that support the back.

1. **Front squat**—performing a squat with the barbell at shoulder height.

2. **Squat clean**—lifting the barbell to shoulder height, then dropping to a squat before pushing barbell above the head with straight arms.

3. **Push jerk**—lifting the barbell from shoulder height to a straight-arms position above the head.

4. **Power snatch**—lifting the barbell from floor to a straight-arms position above the head.

5. **Squat snatch**—lifting the barbell to a straight-arms position above the head but squatting so thighs are flat and parallel to the floor.

5 of the Deadliest Disease Outbreaks in HISTORY

Most diseases can be contained before they spread. But some have spread so quickly that they killed huge numbers of people before they could be stopped. Here are some of the worst in history.

2

The **Black Death** was a plague that broke out in Europe, Africa, and Asia in 1346. By 1353, millions of people had died —maybe as many as 200 million. It is now thought to have been caused by a virus rather than bacteria.

1 **HIV/AIDS** is a disease that attacks the body's immune system, so that the body can no longer fight off other diseases. Since it was identified in 1981, it has killed more than 36 million people. There are now successful treatments.

3

In 1918, **influenza** spread across the world affecting 500 million people. Two in ten people who caught it died. The strangest thing about this flu was that it didn't affect children or the weak, it killed perfectly healthy adults.

4 In AD 541, when the world was a lot less populated, the **Plague of Justinian**, probably an outbreak of bubonic plague, killed half of Europe in a single year—about 25 million people. It was spread by fleas on rats.

5

For two years, from 1956 to 1958, a **flu** that originated in China swept through eastern Asia and the United States, killing around 2 million people.

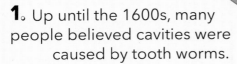

4 Historical Dentistry Facts

1. Up until the 1600s, many people believed cavities were caused by tooth worms.

2. Antony van Leeuwenhoek (1632–1723) was a Dutch scientist who used the newly invented microscope to look at scrapings from people's teeth—and identified oral bacteria for the first time (though he didn't call them that).

3. Drilled teeth more than 7,500 years old have been found in Pakistan—the oldest evidence of dentistry discovered so far.

4. People in the past often had better teeth than people today, despite a shortage of dentists in most parts of the world, because they ate far fewer sugary foods.

4 CAR-DRIVING Skills

It takes most people a long time to learn how to drive. As well as lots of practice and a good teacher, you'll need all of the following:

1. Good hand-eye coordination
2. Quick reflexes (hands and feet)
3. Concentration
4. Clear vision, including peripheral

7 ANIMALS That Are the Same Height as an Average Human

The average height is about 5 ft. 7 in. (1.7 m) for a man and 5 ft. 3 in. (1.6 m) for a woman. When you're fully grown you could be eye-to-eye with one of these animals.

1. Gorilla
4 ft. 7 in. to 5 ft. 11 in.
(1.4 to 1.8 m)

2. Llama
about 5 ft. 7 in.
(1.7 m)

3. Dairy cow
about 5 ft. 7 in.
(1.7 m)

4. Horse
about 5 ft. 7 in.
(1.7 m)

4 Awful CURES for the BLACK DEATH

This disease wiped out half of Europe, and perhaps it wasn't surprising, considering what the doctors of the time were prescribing as cures . . .

1. Urine bath

Sufferers bathed in the pee of uninfected people and even had a glass or two to drink.

2. Poop paste

Cuts were made in the sufferer's skin, and sealed with a paste made of herbs and human poop.

3. Fart inhaling

The disease was thought to be caused by deadly vapors, so this cure used another nasty vapor—farts! People were encouraged to collect their farts in a jar and take regular whiffs to ward off the plague.

4. Chicken rub

Shave a chicken's bottom and stick it under your armpit—those were the instructions. Often, the chickens got sick and then spread their infected parasites.

5. White rhino
about 5 ft. 7 in.
(1.7 m)

6. Red kangaroo
about 5 ft. 7 in.
(1.7 m)

7. Hippopotamus
about 4 ft. 11 in.
(1.5 m)

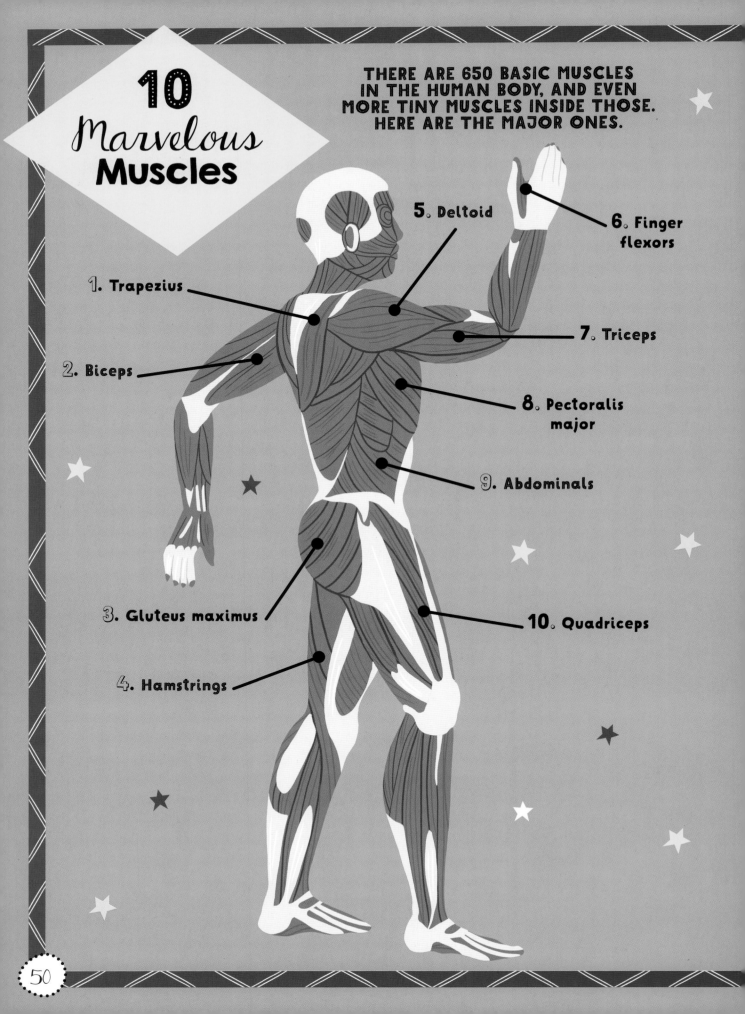

10 Marvelous Muscles

THERE ARE 650 BASIC MUSCLES IN THE HUMAN BODY, AND EVEN MORE TINY MUSCLES INSIDE THOSE. HERE ARE THE MAJOR ONES.

1. Trapezius
2. Biceps
3. Gluteus maximus
4. Hamstrings
5. Deltoid
6. Finger flexors
7. Triceps
8. Pectoralis major
9. Abdominals
10. Quadriceps

8 Facts About Heartbeats

1. Your heart beats about 115,000 times each day.

2. A healthy heartbeat rate is usually around 70 beats per minute when the body is at rest, but can be anywhere from 60 to 100.

3. A pulse is a surge of blood as it is pumped around the body. It can be felt if you hold your finger against the inside of your wrist, the side of your neck, or the top of your foot.

4. The beating sound of your heart is caused by the valves inside the heart opening and closing.

5. You can measure your heartrate by holding your finger against your pulse and counting how many pulses you feel in the space of a minute.

6. Heartrate can be affected by all sorts of things, including exercise, whether you're feeling anxious or calm, and the temperature.

7. The heart can continue beating even when it's disconnected from the body.

8. A woman's heart beats slightly faster than a man's heart.

5 Unique Paralympic Sports

1. Sitting volleyball
Like volleyball, except the net is much lower, the court is smaller, and athletes sit on their bottoms and move around using the power of their arms.

2. Wheelchair rugby
Four players on each side compete to cross the goal line while holding the ball. Blocking and clashing of wheelchairs is allowed.

3. Goalball
Three-per-side sport played by partially sighted or totally blind players, wearing eyeshades to ensure fair play. The ball is made from hard rubber with bells inside, so players can locate it.

4. Wheelchair basketball
Very similar to basketball, with the same number of players, same size court, and the basket at the same height.

5. Wheelchair tennis
The only difference from ordinary tennis is that the ball is allowed to bounce twice on the court before players hit a return shot.

5 Colors of SNOT

1. **Clear**—this is healthy snot. But if there's lots of it, it could be an allergic reaction.

2. **Green/yellow**—Yuck! You've picked up an infection.

3. **White**—your white blood cells might be working extra hard to fight infection.

4. **Red/pink**—if you blow a lot or too hard, you can break blood vessels in your nose which gives the snot a red or pink tinge.

5. **Black/brown**—snot can be dirty, especially if you live in a big city or have been somewhere especially dusty or dirty.

4 INCREDIBLE FACTS ABOUT STEM CELLS

1. We all have these amazing cells growing in our bone marrow—the soft substance found in the center of large bones.

2. Most cells in the human body have a particular function, but stem cells can turn into all sorts of other specialized cells, such as bone, nerve, muscle, or skin cells.

3. Scientists hope to test out the safety of drugs and treatments on specialized stem cells instead of using humans or animals.

4. Stem cells can be transplanted into someone whose own cells have been damaged by cancer or its treatment, and new uses for stem cells are being discovered all the time.

5 Special Powers

There are people with amazing abilities. Some are naturally talented, others learn their special skill—and for some it's a mixture of both.

1. Tetrachromats—most of us can see 1 million colors, but tetrachromats have an extra type of the vision receptors in the eye called cone cells and can see 100 million colors.

2. Perfect pitch—someone with perfect pitch can identify any musical note. Hit a key on a piano and they'll be able to tell you if it's B flat or F sharp.

3. Natural navigators—some people know exactly what direction they are traveling in without a compass or a map. This is probably a learned skill, but not everyone can learn it.

4. Supertasters—most people have between 8,000 and 10,000 taste buds, but some people have even more, which means flavors and tastes are much stronger. They often become professional tasters for food companies.

5. Bat powers—bats use echolocation (bouncing soundwaves off surfaces and listening to the echo to "hear" their surroundings) and some humans are able to do this too. A blind man named Daniel Kish is famous for his wild bike rides, where he uses tongue clicks and echolocation to navigate.

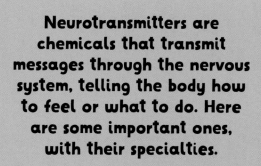

5 NEUROTRANSMITTERS

Neurotransmitters are chemicals that transmit messages through the nervous system, telling the body how to feel or what to do. Here are some important ones, with their specialties.

1. Acetylcholine: muscle contraction, heart rate, digestion, and memory

2. Norepinephrine: feelings of excitement, learning, and mood changes

3. Serotonin: feel-good emotions, sleep, and eating

4. Dopamine: controlling movement and experiencing pleasure

5. Endorphin: controlling pain

5 *Facts* **About** **MARATHONS**

This long-distance race is all about endurance. It's an Olympic sport, a World Athletics event, and popular with amateurs, too. There are around 800 marathons worldwide every year.

1. The name comes from a Greek town and the site of the Battle of Marathon between the Greeks and the Persians in 490 BCE. A Greek runner named Pheidippides ran a long distance to ask for help before the battle, and afterward the Greek army marched quickly back from Marathon to Sparta.

2. The distance is 26.2 miles (42.2 km) long, similar to the distance between Marathon and Athens.

3. The fastest marathon so far was run in 1 hour 59 minutes and 40 seconds, set in 2019 in Vienna by Kenyan runner, Eliud Kipchoge.

4. The biggest and most well-known marathons are those that take place in Tokyo, Boston, London, Berlin, Chicago, and New York City.

5. Most marathons also have wheelchair events if the course is suitable. Boston, USA, doesn't because there are downhill sections of the course.

4 Facts
About Vaccines

When you are vaccinated you are given a tiny dose of the disease you need to be protected from. This allows the body to recognize the disease next time it appears, so your white blood cells are armed and ready to kill it off. Vaccination is one of the most important developments in the history of medicine, and it has saved many millions of lives.

1. Vaccines save up to 3 million lives worldwide each year.

2. Vaccinations are usually given as injections.

3. In the past 60 years, vaccines have helped to rid the world of the deadly disease smallpox, and we are now close to getting rid of polio.

4. Vaccination programs create "herd immunity." That means if most people in a community have been vaccinated against a disease, an unvaccinated person is less likely to catch it.

5 FACTS
About Sight

1. Newborn babies can't see colors, only black, white, and gray.

2. 80 percent of our memories are determined by what we see.

3. About half of the human brain is dedicated to sight.

4. Oily fish, vitamin A, and vitamin C can all help to preserve good eyesight.

5. Pirates believed that wearing gold earrings improved their eyesight.

8 STEPS to Make an Ancient Egyptian Mummy

The Ancient Egyptians believed in an afterlife, and it was important to them that dead bodies were preserved to make them recognizable long after death. So they made dead bodies into mummies—here's a short guide to how they did it.

1. **Remove all internal organs, including the brain.**

2. Leave the internal organs to dry, and put some of them in special jars to go in the burial chamber.

3. **Put the heart back inside the body.**

4. Rinse the body in spices and wine.

5. **Cover the body in salt.**

6. After 40 days, stuff the body with linen or sand to give it back its shape.

7. **After 70 days, wrap the entire body in bandages.**

8. Place inside a sarcophagus (like a coffin).

Straight to Curly in 4 FOLLICLES

Hair grows out of the skin through special pores called follicles. The shape of these pores determines what your hair will be like.

1. Straight—follicle is circular and hair has a direct path out of the skin.

2. **Wavy**—follicle is oval, weakening the hair and making it bend.

3. Curly—follicle is a long, thin, flattened oval, making it weaker on two sides, creating curls.

4. **Corkscrew**—follicle is a flat kidney-bean shape, making hair grow into spirals.

8 POOP Facts

1. **The scientific word for poop is feces (fee-sees).**

2. Poop is what's left over when our bodies have taken all the nutrients from the food we eat.

3. **It also contains stuff that we find hard to digest, such as fats or a tough fiber called cellulose (found in some plants and seeds).**

4. Three quarters of a healthy poop is water.

5. **Poop also contains bacteria we have expelled from our body, so it's important to wash your hands after wiping.**

6. It's fair to say that poop tends to have a strong smell, but if it's particularly stinky it could hint that you ate something your body didn't like, or that your digestive system struggled with.

7. **Poop is brown because of stercobilin—a product created by broken-down, dead red blood cells and bile—which breaks down fats.**

8. Poop that's not brown could be a sign of illness, malnutrition, or infection.

6 COLD Weather Survival Tips

If you find yourself exposed to very low temperatures, knowing what to do can save your life.

1. **Shelter**—pack a good tent! In an emergency, digging a small snow cave can help you survive at night, because packed snow is a great insulator and will trap your body heat.

2. **Drinking plenty of water** is very important in the cold as it maintains good blood flow, which helps to keep you warm.

3. **Make a fire** if you can, for extra warmth. Warm snow in a metal drinking flask to use as a hot-water bottle.

4. **Keep head and neck well protected**—there are many blood vessels near the skin's surface around the head and neck, which can lose heat quickly.

5. **Stay dry**—getting wet will make your body work harder to get warm and use up vital energy.

6. **Keep your fingers and toes warm** to avoid frostbite. Put your fingers under your armpits.

5 ODD Things the Body Does

1. Hiccup
Hiccups happen when we eat or drink too quickly. The stomach swells and irritates the diaphragm—a muscle which contracts in a sudden spasm, causing air to rush into the lungs and the vocal cords to close suddenly, making the "hiccup" sound.

2. Shiver
When it's cold, our body tries to warm up by shaking the muscles, which creates warmth as we use up energy. This is the shivering reflex.

3. Burp
This is the body's way of getting rid of excess air from the stomach, especially after we've gulped down food. The noise comes from the rattling of the epiglottis —a flap that stops food from going down the windpipe—as the air bursts out.

4. Tummy rumble
This is caused by the movement of food, liquid, digestive juices, and air through your intestines. It can be heard more when you're hungry because there's less stuff to muffle the sound!

5. Goosebumps
Tiny hair follicle muscles contract to make the hairs on our skin stand up when we're cold, creating a layer of warmth. It is a leftover reflex from when our ancestors had long body hair.

HOW LONG You Can Live WITHOUT THESE 4 Things

1. Food—**3 weeks**
2. Water—**3 days**
3. Sleep—**10 days**
4. Oxygen—**6 minutes**

5 SIGNS That YOU'RE LOVESICK

Some of the symptoms of being in love are similar to being ill . . .

1. Fluttering in the stomach
2. Increased heartrate
3. Sweaty palms
4. Spinning head
5. Blushing

How We HEAR in 7 STEPS

1. Sounds are actually air waves. They are collected by the outer ear and sent down the ear canal.

2. The sound waves then hit the eardrum, causing it to vibrate.

3. The vibration moves the ear's tiny bones (the smallest bones in the body).

4. The motion of the bones then moves the fluid in the inner ear, which makes tiny hair cells inside bend.

5. The movement of the hair cells is turned into electrical pulses.

6. The electrical impulses are sent to the auditory nerves and into the brain.

7. The brain interprets the impulses as sound.

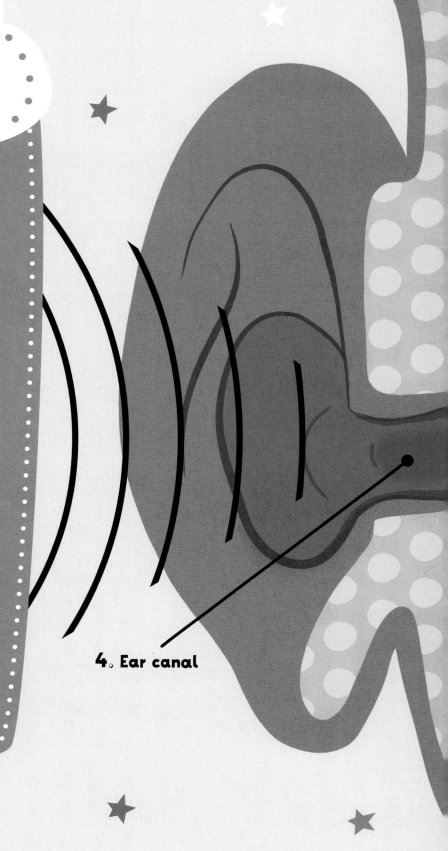

4. Ear canal

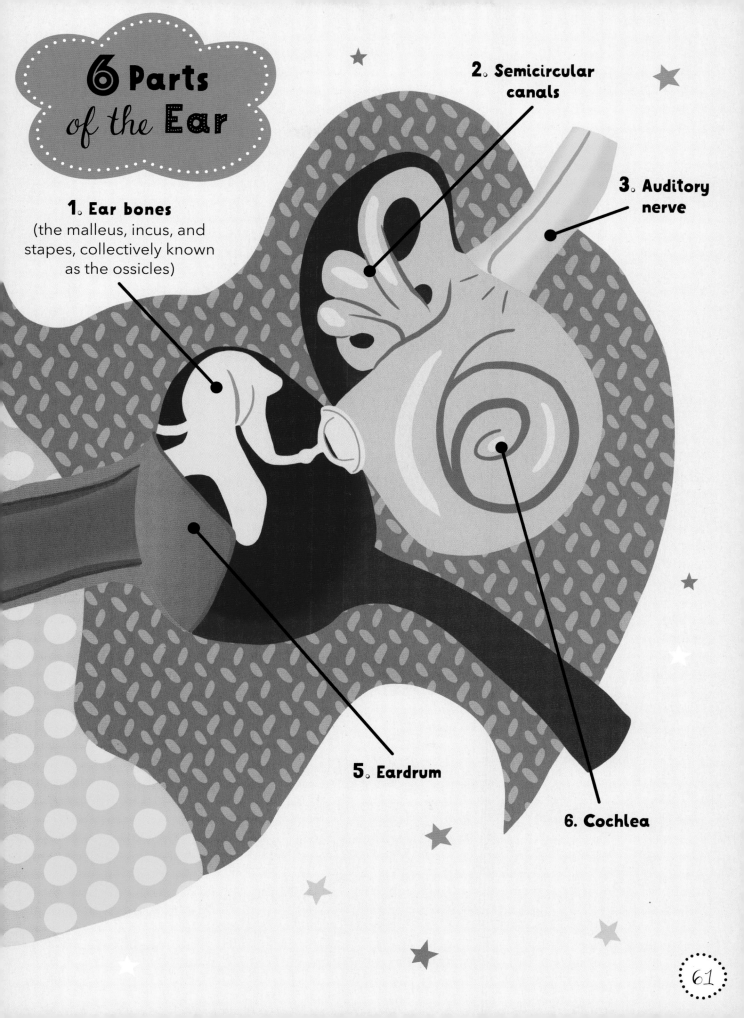

6 Parts of the Ear

1. Ear bones
(the malleus, incus, and stapes, collectively known as the ossicles)

2. Semicircular canals

3. Auditory nerve

5. Eardrum

6. Cochlea

9 Signs of A POOR DIET

What we eat is hugely important to our health, and our bodies can tell us when they're not getting what they need. Eat healthy meals with lots of fruit and vegetables, and keep an eye out for these signs.

1. **Feeling tired**
2. **Dull, brittle, or dry hair**
3. **Fingernails with ridges or dents**
4. **Tooth and gum problems**
5. **Change in poop color and frequency**
6. **Dark-colored urine**
7. **Mood swings**
8. **Bruising easily or cuts that heal slowly**
9. **Picking up illness easily**

5 Deadly Diseases Spread by Insects

Diseases are spread in many ways, but washing your hands won't stop you getting these. You'd be better off with bug spray!

1. **Yellow fever**—a virus transmitted by the bite of certain kinds of mosquito.

2. **Malaria**—caused by parasites, transmitted by the bite of a different kind of mosquito.

3. **Black fever**—caused by parasites and transmitted by sand fly bites.

4. **Sleeping sickness**—caused by parasites and transmitted by tsetse fly bites.

5. **Dengue hemorrhagic fever**—caused by the bite of a mosquito that's bitten someone else with the dengue virus.

4 SMALL THINGS THAT *Really* HURT

These things aren't life-threatening, but they really, really hurt! Why is that?

1. **Stubbing a big toe**
When this happens a huge force is focused on an area of tightly-packed nerve endings, sending a call of alarm to the brain. The pain travels fast because hands and feet are how we explore the world, and we need to know quickly if we're heading into danger.

2. **Paper cut**
When paper slices through your fingertip, which has closely-bunched nerve endings, it sends pain signals to the brain. The cut exposes the nerves to the air and, because there's little or no blood, there's no clotting so the wound stays open. Ouch!

3. **Hitting the funny bone**
When you bash the tip of your elbow, you're also hitting the ulnar nerve that sits in a groove of the bone with no protection. The shock of hitting it can cause tingling all the way down to the little finger it's connected to.

4. **Something in your eye**
It is vital that the eye stays clean and undamaged to protect our vision, so the front surface of the eye carries many tiny nerve cells to protect it. As soon as a bit of grit gets in, the pain it causes drives us to get it out as quickly as we can!

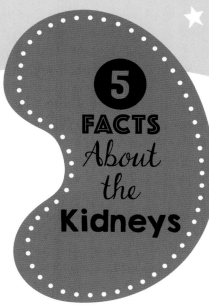

5 FACTS *About the* Kidneys

1. The kidneys are two bean-shaped, fist-sized organs that sit below the ribs. Their job is to remove waste and extra fluid from the body.

2. Each kidney is made up of about a million nephrons. These filter the blood, sending nutrients back to the body and removing waste, which is sent to the bladder.

3. All your blood flows through the kidneys and is filtered by them about 60 times every day.

4. Kidneys make hormones that help make red blood cells and control blood pressure.

5. When kidneys don't work any more, patients have to be connected to a dialysis machine that cleans their blood.

6. Kidneys produce vitamin D, which helps us absorb calcium to keep bones and teeth healthy and strong.

6 STRANGE THINGS
That HAVE TURNED UP INSIDE HUMANS

1. **A nail**—when his nail-gun misfired, a builder from America had the unfortunate experience of having one lodged in his brain. It was successfully removed.

2. **A swordfish bill**—a woman who was snorkeling in Greece was attacked by a swordfish and only discovered later that a bit of its "sword" was lodged in her spine.

3. **Magnets**—an eight-year-old girl swallowed around thirty magnets after thinking they were candies, and had to have them removed from her stomach.

4. **A fork**—an Israeli woman who thought she'd swallowed a cockroach tried to spear it with a fork. But the fork slipped, and she had to have that removed too!

5. **A growing pea plant**—an American man was eating peas when one went down the wrong way and lodged in his lung, where it started to grow!

6. **Ball of human hair**—a teenager with a bad hair-chewing habit went to the hospital with stomach pains. They removed a whopping 11-pound (5-kg) hair ball.

4 Hilarious BODY Jokes

1. **What do you call a skeleton that sleeps all day?**
Lazy bones!

2. **What has a bottom at the top?**
Your legs!

3. **What did one eye say to the other?**
Between you and me, something smells!

4. **What is a blister's favorite play?**
Pus in boots!

5 FACTS
About Eyebrows

1. Eyebrows catch sweat and dirt that trickles down from our foreheads.

2. **Eyebrows give us character. Without eyebrows it is harder to identify a face.**

3. Eyebrows are expressive. We use them to show anger, surprise, and confusion. Some people can raise just one, when they want to show that they are questioning something.

4. **Each eyebrow contains around 250 hairs. The hairs have a lifespan of about four months, and when they fall out new ones grow in their place. Stress can cause them to grow more slowly or not at all.**

5. While some say that eyebrows joined together in the middle are funny-looking, the monobrow has a place in history—many cultures thought they were a sign of intelligence.

5 Historical EYEBROW FASHIONS

1. **Ancient Egyptian men and women wore a lot of dark kohl eye makeup, to emphasize both eyes and eyebrows.**

2. For the Ancient Greeks, the monobrow was a sign of beauty for women. Women sometimes colored their brows with black incense.

3. **The Ancient Romans also believed monobrows to be beautiful, and also a sign of intelligence.**

4. In the Middle Ages, many women plucked their eyebrows to emphasize their foreheads—it was considered beautiful to have a large, domed forehead.

5. **In the 20th and 21st centuries, heavy brows and plucked brows have gone in and out of fashion.**

9 POPULAR Hair Styles

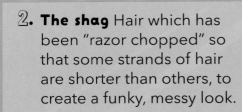

Through the ages people have worn extravagant wigs and extensions, cut, curled, and straightened their hair, and made it into interesting shapes. Here are a few of the popular styles people have worn in the past, and some we still do.

1. The mullet Popular in the 1980s, mullets had short sides, a long back, and a fringe that was either very short or longer and fluffed up.

2. The shag Hair which has been "razor chopped" so that some strands of hair are shorter than others, to create a funky, messy look.

3. Gelled spikes In the 1990s people began to use lots of hair products such as gel or mousse. It was used in shorter hair to create stiff spikes.

4. The pixie crop Cut very short and often with flicks of hair brushed forward onto the face, this cute cut has been popular since the 1960s.

5. **The Farrah Fawcett** Farrah was an American actress famous in the 1970s for her golden locks. Her hair was parted in the middle and flicked away from the face like wings, then held in place with lots of hairspray.

6. **The beehive** In the 1960s it was fashionable to back-comb women's hair so it stood up. It was then fashioned into a large, beehive-shaped bulge.

7. **Cornrows** This traditional African style of braiding is created by plaiting the hair very close to the scalp in rows.

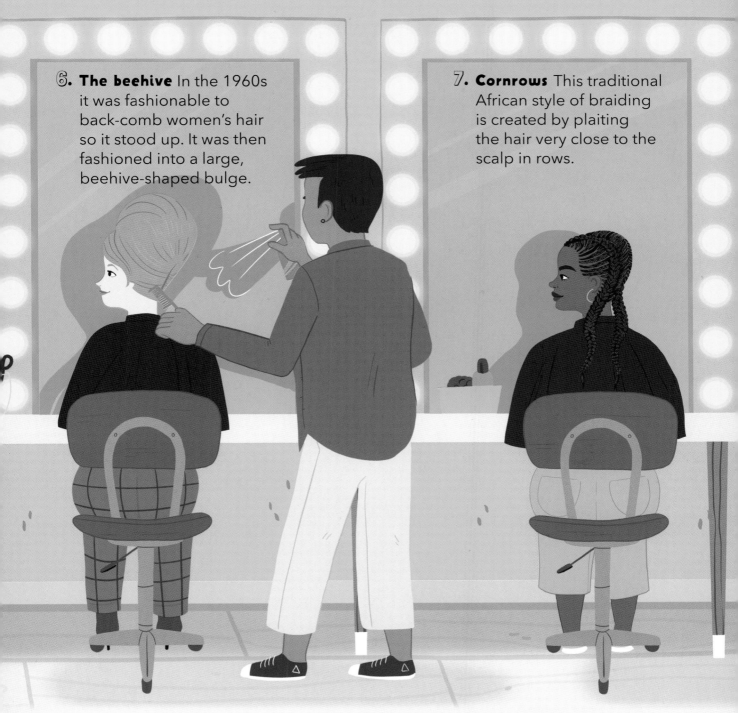

8. **The mop top** Made famous by pop band The Beatles, the hair on top of the head is kept longer than the back and sides, creating a "mop" effect.

9. **The bun** For people with long hair, the old-fashioned bun has become very popular again—either as a scruffy knot at the back, or a smooth, sleek donut placed high on the head.

7 Animals Most Deadly to People

Some animals and insects carry all sorts of nasty bacteria, viruses, venom, and parasites! These are the most dangerous, listed with the approximate number of deaths they cause per year.

1. Mosquito—1 million
Certain mosquitos carry malaria, and mosquitos spread other deadly diseases too, such as yellow fever and dengue fever.

2. Snakes—100,000
Venomous snake bites can kill fast if not treated.

3. Ascaris roundworms—60,000
These worms block the digestive system, causing malnutrition.

4. Dogs—60,000
If a dog is affected with the rabies virus, a bite becomes deadly.

5. Assassin bugs—10,000
These bugs carry Chagas disease, a deadly parasite.

6. Freshwater snails—10,000
Snails can carry schistosomes, parasitic worms.

7. Tsetse flies—1,000
They spread the fatal disease known as sleeping sickness.

6 FACE Shapes

Figure out which of these shapes fits your face.

1. **Round**—the length and width of the face are similar, with a curved jawline.

2. **Square**—length and width measurements are similar, with a strong, sharp-angled jawline.

3. **Oblong**—length of the face is longer than the width.

4. **Diamond**—the length of the face is longer than the width, and the length of the jawline (measured across the face from 3/4 inch or 2 cm below the ears, where you can feel your lower jawbone) is smaller than the width of the cheekbones. The chin is pointed.

5. **Oval**—length of the face is longer than the width of cheekbones, and the forehead measurement is longer than the jawline. The jaw is curved.

6. **Triangular**—the measurement across the jawline is longer than the measurement across the cheekbones, and the forehead is smaller still. The length doesn't matter for a triangular face.

5 Ways to WIN an ARM WRESTLE

Arm-wrestling is a popular tabletop competition of strength, although it's also about technique. Here are some moves to improve your chances!

1. **To gain extra force, position yourself so your dominant foot is closer to your opponent.**

2. Keep your wrestling arm centered in front of you, with your elbow on the table about 3-4 inches (7–10 cm) away from your chest. This allows you to use your shoulder strength as well.

3. **Keep your knuckles as high as possible in the grip. If your hand is positioned slightly above theirs, you can exert more force downward on their arm.**

4. Slowly curl your palm inward to weaken your opponent's wrist.

5. **Make a quick, surprise move on a stronger opponent as soon as the match starts.**

7 REASONS to VOMIT

1. Tummy bug

A virus or bacterial infection that irritates the intestines and lining of the stomach.

2. Motion sickness

Both our eyes and ears detect when the body is moving around. But when there is a lot of fast movement, the brain is bombarded with lots of mixed signals, making you feel dizzy and sick.

3. Morning sickness

Changing levels of hormones and blood sugar can make pregnant women feel sick or vomit in the morning.

4. Food poisoning

When food has gone bad or contains poison the body will try to get rid of it, fast!

5. Concussion

A bang to the head can upset a lot of the signals flying around inside your brain. This can make you feel dizzy and throw up what you last ate.

6. Bad smell

Our brains are programmed to detect substances which might be harmful to us. If your nose and brain pick up a bad smell, this may trigger you to vomit, in case it came from something you ate.

7. Sympathy sick

Hearing or seeing someone else vomit can make you sick. This is possibly your body getting rid of stomach contents in case you ate the same thing. Or it may trigger memories of being sick in the past—which makes you vomit again.

7 WORDS for vomiting

Spewing

Upchucking

Throwing up

Barfing

Blowing chunks

Hurling

Puking

4 Strange Sensations

1. Pins and needles
When you put extra pressure on a part of the body such as the feet or hands, that pressure may cut off the blood supply to the nerves, causing a spiky, tingling sensation. The feeling usually disappears within minutes.

2. "Dead" limbs
Like pins and needles, but when the blood supply is cut off for a long time—during sleep, for instance. It takes longer for the blood to return and the nerves to settle down. In the meantime, the limb feels numb.

3. Cramping
Cramping is a sudden contraction of a muscle—calf muscles may tighten or toes may suddenly curl, which can be very painful. Being in one position for too long, muscle strain, and dehydration can cause cramping, but in many cases no one knows exactly why it happens.

4. Twitching eye
When an eyelid or the rim of the eye suddenly twitches it's a strange feeling. The spasms go away on their own, but tiredness, too much caffeine, or stress are thought to trigger it.

3 ELECTRIFYING FACTS

Everything we do is controlled by electrical signals running through our bodies. Without electricity our bodies and brains wouldn't work.

1.
The electricity in the body doesn't flow along nerves like an electrical wire. It jumps from nerve cell to nerve cell until it reaches its destination.

2.
After death, the electricity in the body enters the surrounding environment through heat or radiation.

3.
Electricity passes through our bodies easily, so if we come into contact with live electricity outside our body it can damage the heart and the brain.

8 Types of Teeth in an Adult Mouth

1. **Central incisors**—cutting

2. **Lateral incisors**—cutting

3. **Cuspids or canines**—gripping and tearing

4. **First premolars**—tearing and crushing

5. **Second premolars**—tearing and crushing

6. **First molars**—grinding

7. **Second molars**—grinding

8. **Wisdom teeth** (don't always appear)—grinding

6 Facts
About Joints

1. **Joints are formed where two or more bones meet.**

2. Most joints are held together by tough tissue called ligaments.

3. **A hinge joint works like a door—the joints in fingers and toes are hinge joints, for example.**

4. A ball-and-socket joint is when a bone with a ball-shaped end rotates inside the cup-shaped end of an adjoining bone—the leg bone fitting into the socket in the pelvis is a ball-and-socket joint.

5. **Joints sometimes come apart, which is known as dislocation. It can be painful but it's easy to put right.**

6. Joints that are damaged can be replaced with stainless steel or plastic copies.

3 Body Part PHOBIAS

1. **Pogonophobia—fear of beards**

2. Genuphobia—fear of knees

3. **Omphalophobia—fear of navels**

10 PARTS of Your Body You Didn't Know THERE Was a Special WORD for

1. **Acnestis**—the spot between your shoulder blades

2. **Canthus**—the outside corner of your eye

3. **Frenulum**—the bit under your tongue attached to the floor of your mouth

4. **Glabella**—the area between your eyebrows

5. **Gnathion**—the bit of your chin that sticks out

6. **Lanula**—the white half-moon at the base of your fingernails

7. **Perlicue**—the L-shaped space between your thumb and index finger

8. **Philtrum**—the groove between the nose and upper lip

9. **Rasceta**—the lines crossing the inside of the wrist

10. **Tragus**—the nub of cartilage at the front of your ear

3 Types of TEARS

Our eyes water because of the lacrimal system, which produces tears. The liquid is thicker than water and even contains antibacterial and pain-killing substances! But not all tears are the same . . .

1. Emotional Tears

Crying is soothing, so strong emotions such as sadness or joy can trigger the lacrimal system to make tears and calm you down.

2. Basal Tears

Keep your eyeballs from drying out.

3. Reflex Tears

Defend eyeballs from irritants such as dirt, smoke, and chemicals (including the gas given off by chopped onions).

9 Facts About TEARS

1. For the first month of life a baby cries without tears.

2. You can cry in your sleep.

3. Tears never run out, but we produce less of the fluid as we get older.

4. Tears have three layers:
   a) a mucus layer to keep the liquid stuck to our skin
   b) an oily layer to stop it from evaporating
   c) a watery layer to hydrate our eyes

5. Tears are similar to saliva, containing salts, minerals, and proteins.

6. They are visible when they spring from our eyes, but most tears drain out of the eye through a tiny hole in the corner of the eyelid into the back of the mouth and down the throat.

7. Crying can help to relieve pain— it stimulates oxytocin, which is a feel-good chemical.

8. A good cry can help you sleep better.

9. Tears contain a powerful antibacterial substance called lysozyme.

 6 BIGGEST
Things *in* the Body

1. **Biggest bone—the femur,** or thigh bone.

2. **Biggest muscle—the gluteus maximus,** which forms part of your bottom and supports posture.

3. **Biggest vein—inferior vena cava,** which carries blood from the lower half of the body to the heart.

4. **Biggest cell—ovum (egg),** found in women and girls only, needed for reproduction.

5. **Biggest organ—the skin,** which covers and protects the body. The biggest internal organ is the liver, which cleans the blood.

6. **Nerve—the sciatic nerve,** which runs down the thigh.

6 TINIEST
Things *in* the Body

1. **Blood vessels—the capillaries,** which are tiny vessels that deliver blood to your cells.

2. **Cell—sperm cell,** found in men and boys only, needed for reproduction.

3. **Nerve—the trochlear nerve,** which is at the back of the brain, connected to the eye.

4. **Bones—the ossicles** are three bones in the inner ear that vibrate to transmit sound.

5. **Muscle—the stapedius,** which supports the ossicles.

6. **Organ—the pineal gland,** which releases a sleep hormone called melatonin.

6
Facts About the Gut

Ancient peoples understood the importance of what goes on in the gut long ago, and now Western society is starting to realize its importance too!

1. **There are more than 100 million nerve cells in the gut that talk directly to the brain.**

2. Around 70 percent of the immune system, which protects us from disease, is inside the gut.

3. **"Gut flora" is the common term for the collection of good bacteria and microorganisms that are found in the gut.**

4. Gut flora affects mood, heart health, and weight gain, and kills off bad bacteria.

5. **Everybody's gut is unique. Even identical twins' are different.**

6. The gut releases more serotonin—the feel-good hormone—than the brain.

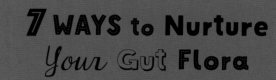

7 WAYS to Nurture Your Gut Flora

1. **Probiotics** (live healthy bacteria) are found in some yogurts or can be taken in a pill.

2. **Fermented foods** such as live kimchi (fermented vegetables) or sauerkraut (fermented cabbage) contain probiotics.

3. **Prebiotics** (foods that encourage probiotics to flourish) include asparagus, bananas, and onions.

4. **Cut down on sugar and artificial sweeteners,** as they can upset the levels of bacteria.

5. **Exercise and healthy eating** improve the variety of bacteria in your gut.

6. **Regular sleep** helps encourage healthy gut flora.

7. **Stop disinfecting so much!** Overuse of cleaning products can damage gut flora.

10 BODY SPECIALISTS

When there's a problem that your regular doctor can't fix with medicine or advice, you are sent to a specialist—an expert in the treatment and care of specific parts of the body.

1. **Cardiologist:** heart

2. Pulmonologist: **lungs**

3. **Dermatologist:** skin

4. Ophthalmologist: **eyes**

5. **Nephrologist:** kidneys

6. Neurologist: brain, spinal cord, and nerves

7. **Orthopedic Surgeon:** bones and joints

8. Hematologist: **blood**

9. **Otolaryngologist:** ear, nose, and throat

10. Gastroenterologist: stomach and digestive system

5 Facts About the Tongue

1. **The tongue is a muscle *and* an organ.**

2. There are between 2,000 and 8,000 taste buds on the tongue.

3. **Saliva dissolves food and releases the chemicals that create flavor. Without saliva the taste buds can't taste!**

4. If a tongue is any other color than pink, it could be a sign of illness or infection.

5. **The jobs a tongue does include tasting, talking, eating, and helping to spit!**

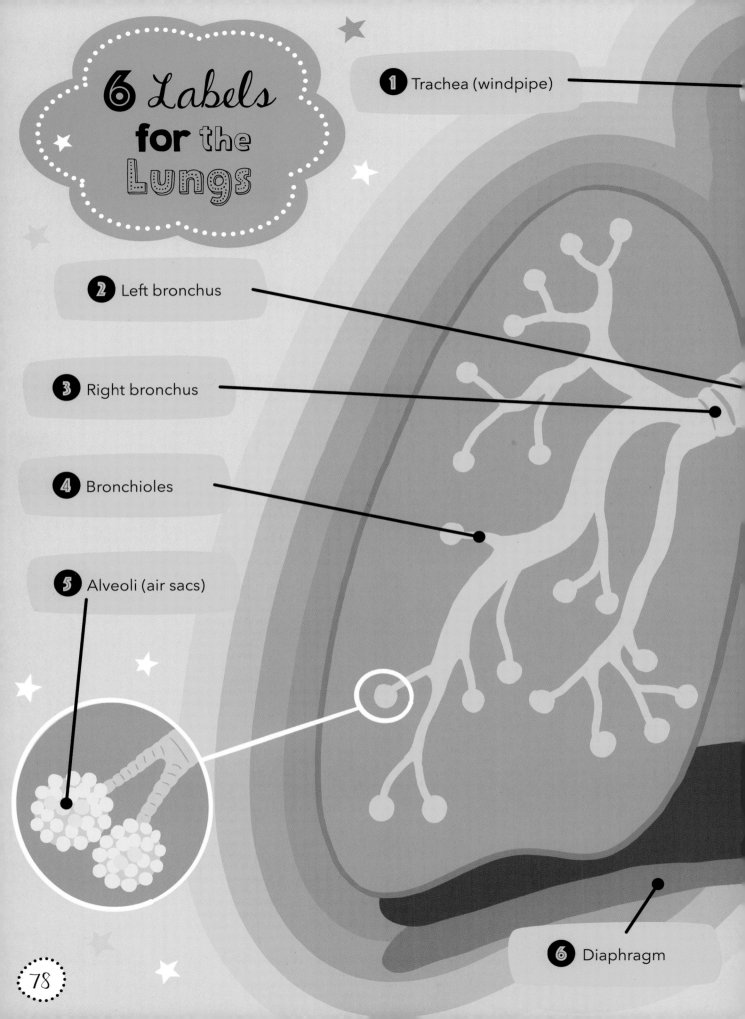

6 Labels for the Lungs

1 Trachea (windpipe)

2 Left bronchus

3 Right bronchus

4 Bronchioles

5 Alveoli (air sacs)

6 Diaphragm

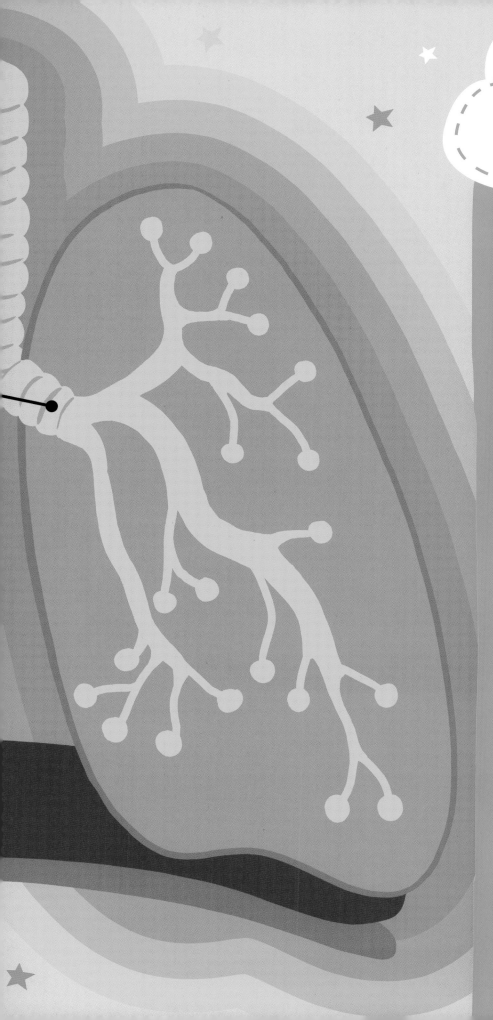

Learn to BREATHE in 8 STEPS

You don't really need to learn how to breathe—you don't even have to think about it. But when you do think about it, it's incredible!

1. Air containing oxygen is drawn in through the mouth or nose.

2. **The air then passes into the trachea.**

3. From the trachea the air enters the left and right bronchi (plural of bronchus).

4. **It filters down through the smaller branches (bronchioles).**

5. The air rushes into the alveoli as the ribs expand.

6. **The tiny blood vessels surrounding the alveoli collect oxygen for the body to use.**

7. The blood vessels pass carbon dioxide and waste gases back into the alveoli.

8. **The carbon dioxide and waste gases are breathed out (exhaled).**

THE ⭐5 Senses

Our senses help us to understand the world around us. There are five main senses, each with its own nervous system, organs, and receptors designed to send information to the brain for processing.

1. Sight
2. Smell
3. Taste
4. Touch
5. Hearing

5 LONGEST Bones

1. **Femur–the thigh bone,** stretches from the hip to the knee, average length 19 inches (48 cm).

2. **Tibia–the shin bone,** connects the ankle to the knee, average length 17 inches (43 cm).

3. **Fibula–the lower leg bone,** runs alongside the tibia, average length 16 inches (40 cm).

4. **Humerus–the upper arm bone,** runs from the shoulder to the elbow, average length 14.5 inches (37 cm).

5. **Ulna–the inner lower arm bone,** connecting the elbow to the wrist, average length 10.5 inches (27 cm).

5 WAYS CHILDREN Are Different from Adults

Apart from obvious differences such as height, age, and experience, there are other ways children differ from grown-ups.

1. Children have **thinner skin**. Anything put on the skin is absorbed more easily.

2. Children **breathe more quickly**.

3. Children have a **larger body surface area** compared to how much they weigh, so they get hot and cold more quickly.

4. Children have **less developed immune systems**, meaning they can pick up illnesses more easily.

5. Children have a **higher metabolic rate**, which means they use up energy faster.

5 EXAMPLES of Acquired Savant Syndrome

Bumping your head isn't good for you, but for a few people it can have surprising benefits. They become instant geniuses!

1. When Orlando L. Serrell from America was 10 years old, he was hit on the head by a baseball. Since then, he can remember exactly what he was doing on any day in the past, including what he had to eat or what the weather was like.

2. Tommy McHugh from Britain suffered bleeding on the brain when he was 51 years old. After that, all he wanted to do was create art and talk in rhyme. By the time he died, he'd covered his entire house in paintings.

3. A young Australian named Ben McMahon went into a coma after he was involved in a car crash. When he woke up he found he could speak Mandarin, one of the languages spoken in China. He'd had a few lessons, but suddenly he was fluent, and Mandarin had replaced English as his first language!

4. Lachlan Connors from America suffered multiple concussions while playing sports, but recovered with a remarkable talent for music. He can now play 13 instruments.

5. Briton Daniel Tammett had an epileptic seizure when he was a young teen. Afterward, he could suddenly work out the trickiest math problems, and was able to pick up languages with surprising speed—he became fluent in Icelandic within a week!

5 Effects of SPACE TRAVEL on the BODY

1. We use our muscles even when we're not doing very much at all, because we have gravity to push against. In space there's no gravity, so astronauts' muscles get weaker. The lack of gravity affects bone mass, too, especially in the pelvis and legs. Astronauts use exercise machines in space to try to make up for it.

2. Because there is no gravity to keep body fluids in the usual places, liquid can travel through the body to different areas. Liquid travels up from the legs and into the face, which causes "skinny legs" and "moon face."

3. Without gravity, the size and shape of the heart changes. The blood isn't pumped around the body efficiently, the heartrate slows, and blood pressure goes down.

4. Earth's atmosphere protects us from space radiation. Without it astronauts can be exposed to ten times more radiation than they're used to. This increases the likelihood of radiation sickness (feeling tired and sick) and of getting cancer.

5. After being in space for some time, it can be hard to walk on solid ground. When they come back down to Earth, many astronauts find the pressure on their feet painful. They also feel dizzy and have trouble staying upright.

The 5 PHASES of Sleep

When we go to sleep there's no such thing as a silent night. Our eyes might be closed, but all sorts of things are going on in our brains and bodies.

1. Light sleep with slow eye movement and relaxed muscles.

2. Eye movement stops and normal, waking brain waves slow down.

3. The brain starts to emit slow delta waves, as we move into deeper sleep.

4. Deep sleep, with no eye or muscle movement—only delta brain waves. This is when the body restores and mends itself.

5. Dreaming, when rapid eye movement (REM) occurs. Breathing becomes faster and shallower as heart rate and blood pressure rise.

4 FACTS About Yoga

1. Yoga is an ancient Indian discipline over 5,000 years old.

2. A female yoga teacher is called a yogini and a male is a yogi.

3. There are over 100 styles of yoga.

4. There are lots of ways yoga can keep you healthy: it helps to boost the immune system, focuses the mind, improves posture, and reduces feelings of anxiety.

7 Simple Yoga Poses

1. DOWNWARD-FACING DOG

2. THE LOTUS POSE

3. THE COBRA POSE

4. THE TREE POSE

5. THE TRIANGLE POSE

6. THE PLANK POSE

7. THE CHILD'S POSE

85

3 Remarkable Body Part Records

1. Longest fingernails on a single hand—358.11 inches (909.6 cm), Shridhar Chillal (India), 2014

2. Widest mouth (unstretched)—6.7 inches (17 cm) across, Francisco Domingo Joaquim (Italy), 2010

3. Most fingers and toes on a living person—31, Kumari Nayak (India), 2020

4 of the WORLD'S STRANGEST and MOST DANGEROUS FOODS

1. Puffer fish
This is a delicacy in Japan, known as fugu, and must be prepared by highly trained chefs. It contains a deadly poison, and if it's not properly cleaned and prepared it can kill!

2. Blood clams
This shellfish carries many viruses. They are boiled fast and eaten right away, but if the viruses aren't killed they can give the eater deadly diseases.

3. Bullfrogs
Eaten whole as a delicacy in several African countries, bullfrogs can be risky to eat because they contain toxins.

4. Hákarl
In Greenland, meat from Greenland sharks is buried for a while then hung up to dry for a few months, after which it's eaten as a stinky, flavorsome snack. But toxins are stored in the flesh, and if the meat hasn't broken down enough while buried, it can be poisonous.

9 Chemical Elements Inside Our Bodies

All of the following elements are found in the body and help to keep it healthy. You might be surprised to know that you contain iron and copper—they're in there somewhere, but in very tiny amounts.

1. Calcium
2. Chromium
3. Cobalt
4. Copper
5. Iron
6. Magnesium
7. Manganese
8. Potassium
9. Sodium

6 Sayings Involving Body Parts from AROUND the WORLD

1. Putting your foot in your mouth (saying the wrong thing—English)

2. Not having hairs on your tongue (being honest/talking frankly—Spanish and Italian)

3. The knife has reached the bone (when someone can't take any more—Romanian)

4. Costing the eyes in your head (costing an unreasonable amount—French)

5. Giving a tooth (swearing something to be true—Russian)

6. Habit is the body's skin (habits are hard to break—Swahili)

3 PHYSICAL Features That MIGHT Affect YOUR LIFE

1. Shorter people tend to live longer.

2. Naturally strong and healthy teeth are light yellow, not pearly white.

3. Redheads are more sensitive to some types of pain—especially toothache—and need more anesthesia during surgery than people with other hair colors.

9 Brainy Facts

1. The human brain is more efficient than the most powerful computer in the world.

2. The brain is made up of neurons—special cells that connect to one another, passing messages. There are around 86 billion neurons in a brain.

3. At two years old, a child's brain is already 80 percent the size of an adult brain.

4. Your brain has reached its full weight at around eight years old, but doesn't stop growing until your mid-20s.

5. If you stretched out the surface of a brain it would be about the size of a pillowcase.

6. The brain generates enough electricity to power a small lightbulb.

7. Nearly 80 percent of the brain is water.

8. The brain is the fattiest organ in the body.

9. Brains crave stimulation, which is why solitary confinement with no entertainment, company, books, or paper and pens is a terrible punishment.

4 CURES FOR HICCUPS

There's no guarantee any of these will work . . .

1. Pull your knees up to your chest and lean forward.

2. Suck a lemon.

3. Eat half a teaspoon of granulated sugar.

4. Drink from the opposite side of the glass.

8 Famous Doctors

1. HIPPOCRATES, 460BC-370BC
Greek physician, known as the father of modern medicine. He realized the importance of diet and studied body functions and diseases. The "Hippocratic Oath" is sworn by some of today's doctors in his honor.

2. ELIZABETH BLACKWELL, 1821-1910
The first British woman to be on the UK medical register and the first woman to receive a medical degree in America. She paved the way for future female doctors.

3. EDWARD JENNER, 1749-1823
Doctor who created the smallpox vaccine. This breakthrough allowed many other vaccines to be developed, changing the course of medicine.

4. HENRY GRAY, 1827-1861
Anatomist and surgeon who published the famous human body textbook, *Gray's Anatomy*.

5. JOSEPH LISTER, 1827-1912
Surgeon who established the use of antiseptic, which prevented infection and saved many lives.

6. THOMAS JOHN BARNARDO, 1845-1905
In his lifetime, this Irish doctor helped around 60,000 poor children, and provided them with education and homes.

7. MAE CAROL JEMISON, 1956-PRESENT
An engineer, doctor, and NASA astronaut, Jemison was the first black woman to travel in space when she served as a medical specialist aboard the Space Shuttle Endeavour in 1992.

8. HELEN B. TAUSSIG, 1898-1986
Cardiologist (heart doctor), famous for her work with children with heart conditions.

HOW a BABY Develops in 12 STAGES

. . . .

1. **1 week:** a fertilized egg fixes itself onto the wall of the uterus, or womb.

2. **4 weeks:** the egg (now called an embryo) has linked itself to the mother's blood supply. The cells of the embryo are dividing and developing.

3. **6 weeks:** the embryo is showing signs of growing legs and is forming a heart and brain.

4. **10 weeks:** the developing baby is now called a fetus. The heart is formed and beating and a face is starting to take shape.

5. **12 weeks:** all the muscles and bones are in place.

6. **16 weeks:** the fetus is starting to move around more and its hands can make a fist.

7. **20 weeks:** the fetus is putting on weight and reacting to noises.

8. **24 weeks:** the organs, such as the heart and lungs, continue to develop.

9. **28 weeks:** the fetus is fully formed, and usually weighs around 2.2 pounds (1 kg).

10. **32 weeks:** the fetus can suck its thumbs and often turns downward, ready for birth.

11. **36 weeks:** the lungs and digestive system are ready to function outside of the mother's womb.

12. **40 weeks:** the baby is ready to be born, although babies are often born two weeks earlier or later.

5 Facts About Chromosomes

1. Chromosomes are tiny structures inside cells, made from DNA and protein.

2. **The information inside chromosomes tells cells what to do.**

3. Chromosomes are shaped like an elongated X, and come in pairs.

4. **Each pair is made up of one chromosome from a person's father, and one from their mother.**

5. Humans have 23 pairs in each cell. They are identical apart from the 23rd pair, called the X/Y pair. This pair decides whether you are male or female—XY in boys, and XX in girls.

5 TOOTHPASTE RECIPES *from* Long Ago

1. **Ancient Egyptian toothpaste included powdered ox hooves, pumice stone, and eggshells, with mint, salt, and dried flowers as flavorings.**

2. Ancient Greek and Roman toothpaste contained crushed bones, oyster shells, charcoal, and bark.

3. **The Ancient Romans used urine to brush their teeth and as a mouthwash to keep teeth clean and sparkling white.**

4. In England in the Middle Ages, toothpaste contained salt, rye flour, and honey.

5. **During the Chinese Song Dynasty, toothpaste was made from poria mushrooms, and herbs and spices were used to freshen the breath.**

4 Technologies to IMPROVE the Human Body

It's only a matter of time before humans are using technology inside their bodies to improve their everyday lives. Here are some human body enhancements that are already being tested.

1. **Magnetic implants in fingers or hands, allowing the wearer to sense electric fields and pick up metal objects.**

2. Digital tattoos that contain personal data and can measure body activity, such as heart rate, and send the information to a computer.

3. **Cyborg antenna—invented by color-blind artist Neil Harbisson—allows people to "view color" with their mind instead of their eyes.**

4. In-skin radio-frequency identification chips allow the user to interact with machines instead of using a password or personal identification number.

3 HAIRY MUSEUMS

1. **Chez Galip Hair Museum, Avanos, Turkey**—more than 16,000 locks of women's hair are on display.

2. **Leila's Hair Museum, Missouri, USA**—exhibits wreaths and jewelry made from human hair.

3. **Japanese Coiffure Museum, Kyoto, Japan**—miniature wigs show more than a hundred Japanese hairstyles from throughout history, as well as hair ornaments and combs.

22 Bones in the SKELETON

There are 206 bones altogether in an adult human body. These are some of the most important ones to know about.

11. Cranium (skull)

12. Mandible (jawbone)

13. Clavicle (collarbone)

14. Sternum (breastbone)

15. Ulna (part of forearm)

16. Pelvis

17. Sacrum

1. Ribs

2. Humerus (upper arm bone)

3. Vertebrae (spine)

4. Radius (part of forearm)

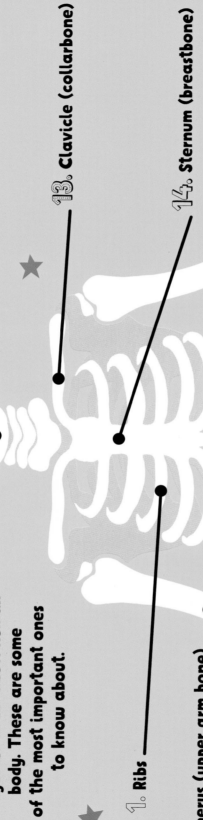
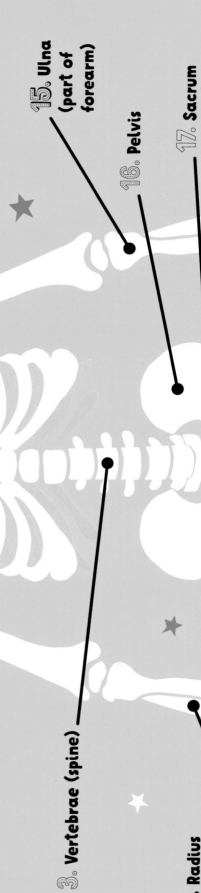

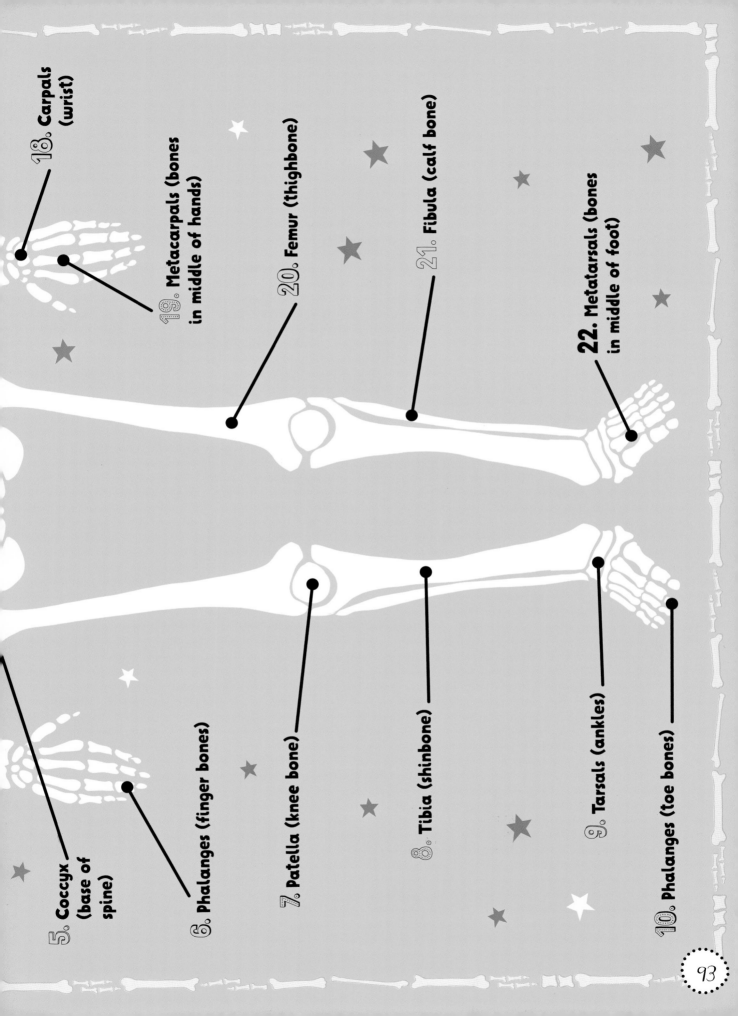

18. Carpals (wrist)

19. Metacarpals (bones in middle of hands)

20. Femur (thighbone)

21. Fibula (calf bone)

22. Metatarsals (bones in middle of foot)

5. Coccyx (base of spine)

6. Phalanges (finger bones)

7. Patella (knee bone)

8. Tibia (shinbone)

9. Tarsals (ankles)

10. Phalanges (toe bones)

93

4 Muscly Gymnastics Events

1. **Rings**—uses triceps, biceps, pectorals, deltoids, lats, shoulders.
2. **Balance beam**—uses core and leg muscles.
3. **Parallel bars L-sit**—uses triceps, shoulders, abdominals, and core.
4. **Vault**—uses core, shoulders, triceps, leg muscles.

Bruises Explained in 4 Colors

Bruises appear when you bump a part of your body. They can turn some interesting colors . . .

1. Red
Immediate bruises are usually red because of the blood that collects under the skin. The darker the skin, usually the darker the color.

2. Blue, purple, and black
As the pool of blood under the skin loses oxygen, the bruise turns darker.

3. Yellow and green
The blood cells in the bruise are broken down to be reabsorbed into the body. This process creates substances including biliverdin and bilirubin, which give an old bruise its green and yellowy colors.

4. Light brown
As they fade, bruises turn a pale brown, more visible on fairer skin.

5 UNIQUE Body Features

1. Tongue
Every tongue has its own shape and texture of bumps and ridges. It can be an even better identifier than a fingerprint.

2. Fingerprints and toeprints
The skin on our fingers and toes have patterns made up of ridges and whorls that are unique to each person.

3. Iris
The iris is the colored part of the eye. It has patterns made up of pits and ridges, with a mixture of colors and shades. It can even have blotches and freckles. Every single iris is one of a kind, even in a pair of eyes belonging to one person.

4. Lip print
Like a fingerprint, lips also have a pattern of ridges unique to their owner.

5. Ears
The curled rim of the ear is yours and yours alone. These ear formations are so unique, technology is being developed so that in the future you may be able to unlock your phone just by holding it to your ear.

5 Ways to Decorate the Body

People have decorated their bodies for thousands of years. There are all sorts of ways to make your skin stand out (sometimes literally).

1. Tattoos
Permanent marks are made by injecting ink into the second layer of the skin with a needle. Tattooists draw a design on the skin—words, patterns, or pictures—and trace it with a fast-moving tattoo machine that pushes the inky needle in and out at great speed.

2. Piercings
A needle is passed through the skin and the hole filled with a stud, bar, or hoop. Over time, the skin heals around the object and the hole in the skin is permanent.

3. Henna
The dye made from the henna tree causes staining and can be used on the skin to create a temporary tattoo that lasts one to three weeks.

4. Scarification
The skin is cut, and the wound is burned or filled with ink. Depending on the process, the healed scars are either raised or etched.

5. Subdermal implants
Objects are inserted under the skin so that they can be seen or felt. Some people have bumps and studs. Some even have horns!

7 Fatty Facts

Our bodies need fat, but some kinds of fat are much better for us than others.

1. Fat is a source of essential fatty acids that help the body to absorb vitamins. Vitamins A, D, and E cannot be absorbed without it.

2. Monounsaturated and polyunsaturated are good fats. They come mainly from vegetables, nuts, seeds, and fish and can raise our levels of good cholesterol—a waxy type of fat made by the liver.

3. Cholesterol is needed by the body to build cells and do other jobs, but too much can clog up your arteries. Some types of cholesterol are more healthy than others.

4. Omega-3 fatty acids—found in eggs and fish—can help prevent heart disease, lower blood pressure, and raise levels of good cholesterol.

5. Saturated fats come from animal fat, some kinds of dairy, and are also present in coconut and palm oil. They are generally less healthy than unsaturated fats.

6. Trans fats are artificially made and used in processed foods, like cookies, to increase shelf life and flavor. But they are not healthy and can cause problems like heart disease so they are not used in some countries.

7. If a fat is solid at room temperature, it is more likely to be saturated fat, whereas monounsaturated and polyunsaturated fats, such as olive oil, are usually liquid.

6 IMPORTANT Medical Discoveries

We all benefit from these discoveries, and many millions of people wouldn't be alive without them.

1. Germ theory (the idea that germs can cause disease) has led to effective ways of preventing and treating infections and illness.

2. Anesthesia means patients don't need to feel pain during operations.

3. Vaccination stops people from getting different infections, saving many millions of lives.

4. Antibiotics kill bacteria and stop infections.

5. The discovery of DNA has created new possibilities for medical treatments.

6. Medical imaging, which began with X-rays, allows doctors to see what's going on underneath the skin.

7 FACTS About Blood

1. Blood contains red blood cells, white blood cells, and platelets.

2. Red blood cells are made in bone marrow and carry oxygen around the body. They contain haemoglobin which contains iron and reacts with oxygen to make the red color.

3. White blood cells combat disease. There are five different types.

4. Platelets help the blood to clot when the skin is cut so that you don't keep bleeding.

5. The blood cells float around in plasma, a yellowy liquid that contains nutrients.

6. Not all blood is the same—there are eight main blood groups.

7. Hospitals rely on people donating blood to help with operations and transfusions, which is when someone needs their blood replaced.

4 THINGS that Make Up BLOOD

1. Red blood cells
2. Platelets
3. White blood cells
4. Plasma

5 FACTS About DNA

1. **DNA stands for deoxyribonucleic acid.**

2. DNA is a chemical made up of two long molecules that spiral around each other in a shape called a double helix.

3. **DNA is held inside the nucleus of every single cell in the body.**

4. DNA holds all the information required to grow a living thing.

5. **DNA is used in police work to help solve crimes. Because it is in every cell and unique to each person, even a single hair can identify a suspect.**

6 THINGS About GENES

1. Genes are sections of DNA.

2. Genes carry information that determines who we are and what we look like.

3. Every gene has a different job. Some genes tell cells to make proteins. Some proteins power muscles, others fight disease, make fingernails, affect hair color, and so on.

4. Each cell in the human body contains over 40,000 genes.

5. Genes come in pairs—we inherit one copy from each of our parents, which is why we may share physical features, such as eye or hair color, with them.

6. The genes that are passed on are random, which is why we may not look like our siblings, for example.

6 STEPS to HAPPINESS

Everyone is unhappy some of the time, but these tips might help to keep a smile on your face.

1. **Be positive**—it's important to think of things that are good in your life and not to dwell on the negatives.

2. **Focus**—sometimes life can be overwhelming, so it's good to focus on a single thing for a moment and give it all of your attention.

3. **Get moving**—exercise releases endorphins, which are feel-good hormones, and can release stress and strengthen the heart. Just going for a brisk walk can help.

4. **Eat healthily**—what goes on in the gut can affect your mood.

5. **Talk about it**—if there's something bothering you, talk to someone you trust and feel comfortable with.

6. **Sleep well**—go to bed at a sensible time and stay away from screens for an hour before you turn out the light.

3 Medieval Cures for Stomach Ache

1. Rub a mixture of wax, oil, and pitch (a thick black liquid used for waterproofing ships) onto the stomach.

2. Apply leeches to the stomach (applying leeches was a common cure for a lot of illnesses).

3. Ask a small child or dog to sit on your stomach.

③ MARATHON SWIMS

1. The Cook Strait, between New Zealand's North and South Islands: **13.7 miles (22 km)**

2. The Catalina Channel, between the coast of California and Santa Catalina Island: 20.2 miles (32.5 km)

3. The English Channel, between England and France at their closest points: 21.1 miles (34 km)

④ Swimming Strokes

These four swimming strokes are the ones used in the Olympic Games and other competitions.

1. Freestyle, also known as front crawl, which is the fastest stroke.

2. Butterfly, the second-fastest stroke, but you'll need to be very fit to swim more than a few lengths.

3. Backstroke, the only stroke swum with the head facing upward.

4. Breaststroke, the most popular swimming stroke but also the slowest.

11 Greetings *from* AROUND *the* World

1. **Shaking hands**
   —Western culture

2. **Rubbing noses**
   —Inuit peoples of the Arctic Circle

3. **Sticking out tongues**
   —Tibetan monks

4. **Placing the forehead on the back of the other's hand**
   —Philippines

5. **Touching foreheads**
   —Hawaii, called "honi"

6. **Kissing cheeks**
   —Western culture

7. **Hugging**
   —worldwide

8. **Bowing**
   —Japan

9. **Pressing noses together**
   —Oman and the United Arab Emirates

10. **Pressing noses and foreheads together**
    —Maori, called "hongi"

11. **Jumping**
    —Maasai people of East Africa

7 Measurements Using Body PARTS

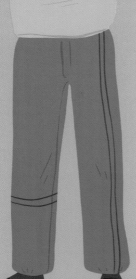

Today we mainly use the metric or imperial systems of measurement, but in the past measurements were based on parts of the body—despite the fact that people come in different sizes. Today some of them are still used, but have a fixed length.

1. **Cubit**—the measurement of a forearm from elbow to fingertip.

2. **Fathom**—the distance between hands of two outstretched arms.

3. **Hairbreadth**—the width of a hair.

4. **Hand**—the width of a hand (still used to measure the height of horses today).

5. **Foot**—a foot's length, now 30.5 cm or 12 inches.

6. **Thumb**—the width of a thumb.

7. **Span**—the distance between the thumb and little finger on an outstretched hand.

9 PHOBIAS that are Hard to Live With

1. Mysophobia—being exposed to germs
2. Somniphobia—falling asleep
3. Ablutophobia—washing
4. Phagophobia—swallowing
5. Agoraphobia—being in a wide open space or going outside
6. Monophobia—being alone
7. Claustrophobia—small or closed spaces
8. Phonophobia—voices
9. Osmophobia—smells

5 Tips for Surviving Desert Heat

1. **Wear a big hat and cover your arms and legs to help keep cool and protected from the Sun.**
2. Ration your water. Take small sips at long intervals.
3. **Eating makes you thirsty, so eat as little as possible.**
4. Move slowly to help conserve energy.
5. **Keep your mouth closed to slow the rate of dehydration from breathing.**

5 BELLY BUTTON Facts

1. **Your belly button is a scar where the umbilical cord that attached you to your mother used to be.**
2. Belly buttons are also known as navels, or as the formal medical term, umbilicus.
3. **There's a Belly Button Festival in the town of Furano, Japan. People paint faces on their bare stomachs and dance through the streets.**
4. Collecting the fluff that gathers in belly buttons can be a hobby. Graham Barker from Australia has the world's largest collection, and an artist named Rachel Betty Case makes tiny teddy bears out of it.
5. **But before you start your own collection, remember that belly buttons are home to a lot of bacteria. The Belly Button Biodiversity Project, run by North Carolina State University, found 1,458 previously undiscovered bacteria in the belly buttons they studied.**

Children Per Family in 18 COUNTRIES

These are some average numbers of children born per family around the world.

1. **Niger**—7.2
2. Somalia—**6.2**
3. **Nigeria**—5.4
4. Afghanistan—**4.55**
5. **Pakistan**—3.35
6. Israel—**2.92**
7. **South Africa**—2.4
8. India—**2.3**
9. Mexico—2.13
10. France—**1.97**
11. United States of America—**1.88**
12. **United Kingdom**—1.87
13. Russia—**1.75**
14. **China**—1.65
15. Canada—**1.56**
16. **Germany**—1.47
17. Spain—**1.39**
18. **South Korea**—1.32

6 Facts About MUSIC and the Brain

1. Playing a musical instrument exercises many parts of the brain, strengthens memory, and improves speed of movement in eyes and hands.

2. Listening to music is a workout too-there's lots of computing going on as the brain makes sense of the notes and their sequences.

3. A chemical called dopamine is released when listening to music you enjoy, spreading a pleasurable feeling.

4. Listening to music can wake you up, decrease anxiety, reduce pain, and speed up healing.

5. Background music that isn't distracting can give creativity a real boost.

6. Music stays in the memory-people with memory loss can often still recall a piece of music long after they've forgotten other familiar things, like names and faces.

8 Horrible Beauty Treatments

1. **Ancient Egyptians used eye makeup made from copper ore and poisonous lead sulfide, which hurt people's eyes.**

2. Ancient Greeks and Romans used cream on their faces that contained lead, which is poisonous and led to lots of health problems.

3. **In the Middle Ages, women drained some of their blood (known as bloodletting) so they would look fragile and pale, which they thought was beautiful!**

4. Italian women in the 15th and 16th centuries, and also women in Victorian Britain, used eye drops to dilate their pupils, which they thought made them look more attractive. The eye drops were made from a poisonous plant, which could cause blindness.

5. **Victorian women ate wafers laced with arsenic to make them pale. Arsenic is a poison and can be fatal.**

6. Victorian women also took pills containing tapeworms, in the hope it would make them slimmer.

7. **As recently as 2007, lots of lipsticks still contained lead!**

8. Mercury is a metal that can damage the skin and make you very ill, yet it's still used today in tiny doses in some beauty products.

4 HISTORICAL Cures for TOOTHACHE

Be very glad for modern dentists!

1. Apply a dead mouse to the affected tooth—Ancient Egyptian cure

2. Chew hot chili peppers—Aztec cure

3. Apply a caterpillar wrapped in red cloth—old Scottish cure

4. Catch a frog at full moon, spit into its mouth, then tell it to go away and take the toothache with it—Ancient Roman cure

6 Facts About the Circadian RHYTHM

1. The circadian rhythm is the internal clock that makes us feel tired at night and awake during the day.

2. **All living things have circadian rhythms, including animals, plants, and even bacteria.**

3. Your circadian rhythm is controlled by a group of nerve cells in the brain called the suprachiasmatic nucleus (SCN).

4. **The SCN controls body temperature and sleepiness, based on the amount of light that your eyes are seeing. That's why screens before bedtime are bad news.**

5. When circadian rhythms are confused it affects the growth of blood vessels and can cause or add to health problems.

6. **Teenagers have a different circadian rhythm from younger children and adults, which makes them want to stay up later and sleep in longer.**

7 FACTS About CALORIES

1. A calorie is a unit of energy. Everything we do uses up calories— even sleeping.

2. If we eat more calories than we burn, we put on weight.

3. Watching television and gaming burns no more calories than sleeping.

4. Exercising burns a lot of calories as the body works harder to pump blood.

5. Elementary school children need 1,600–2,200 calories a day, depending on how active they are.

6. "Empty calories" is a term used to describe foods that provide energy but little or no other useful nutrients.

7. Your metabolism is the rate your body naturally burns calories in order to function.

5 THINGS
About PROSTHETICS

1. A prosthesis is an artificial body part. The first one to be recorded was a big toe on an Egyptian noblewoman!

2. There are prosthetic arms, hands, legs, feet, fingers, toes, ears, noses, and eyes.

3. Typically, a prosthetic arm or leg is made from a strong lightweight material such as carbon fiber, covered with foam padding (for comfort) or flesh-colored plastic.

4. The future of prosthetics is exciting. At the Johns Hopkins University, USA, scientists are developing skin to cover prosthetic hands that can deliver the feeling of touch to the brain.

5. Runners with lower-leg amputation use "blades," which have the advantage of being light and springy.

5 Reasons
Sugar Isn't SWEET

A little bit once in a while is OK, but too much sugar can be very bad for your health.

1. Sugar is addictive, so you want more and more.

2. It can prevent healthy bacteria from growing in your insides.

3. A high-sugar diet raises your risk of lots of different diseases.

4. Eating a lot of sugar can create big mood swings —sudden bursts of energy followed by crashes.

5. Sugar is a major cause of tooth decay.

4 HORRID CURES
for Headaches

1. Ancient Greek doctor Arateus of Cappadocia recommended shaving the head and burning through the skin of the forehead. The patient's bravery was supposed to cure the headache!

2. In the 10th century, Ali ibn Isa al-Kahhal prescribed a dead mole strapped to the head as a cure for a headache caused by eye disease.

3. In 1762, The Dutch Society of Sciences stated that if a slave complained of headache, he or she must touch the head with one hand and an electric eel with the other.

4. Trepanning, the method of boring a hole in the skull to relieve headaches, went on for centuries, and until the 1600s it was quite common.

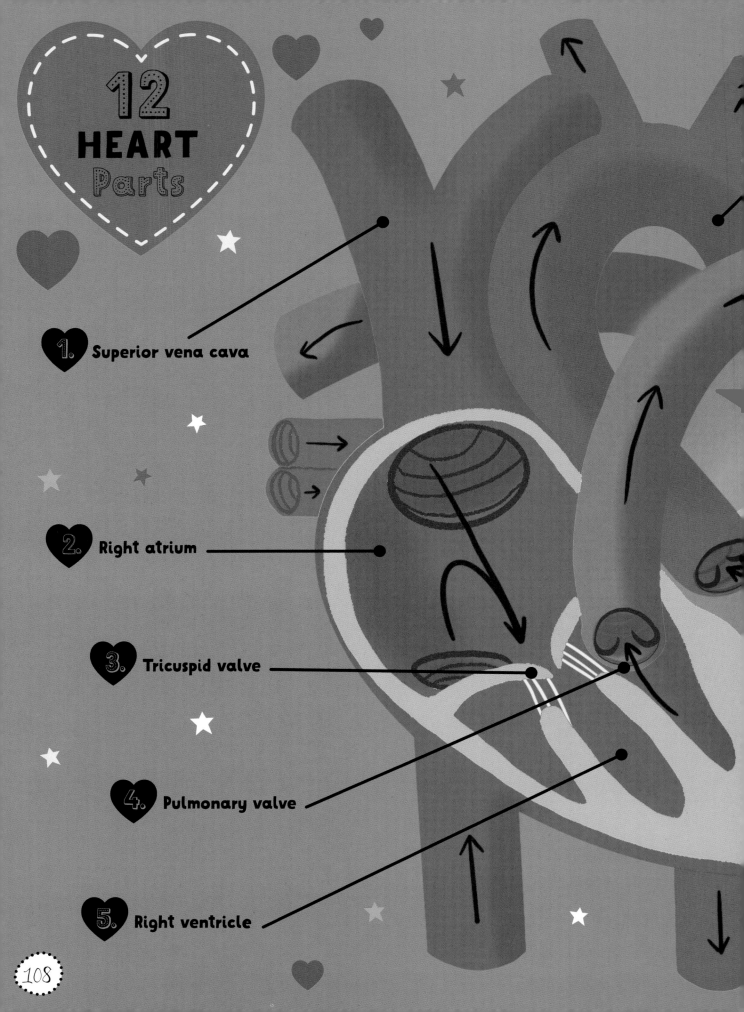

12 HEART Parts

1. Superior vena cava

2. Right atrium

3. Tricuspid valve

4. Pulmonary valve

5. Right ventricle

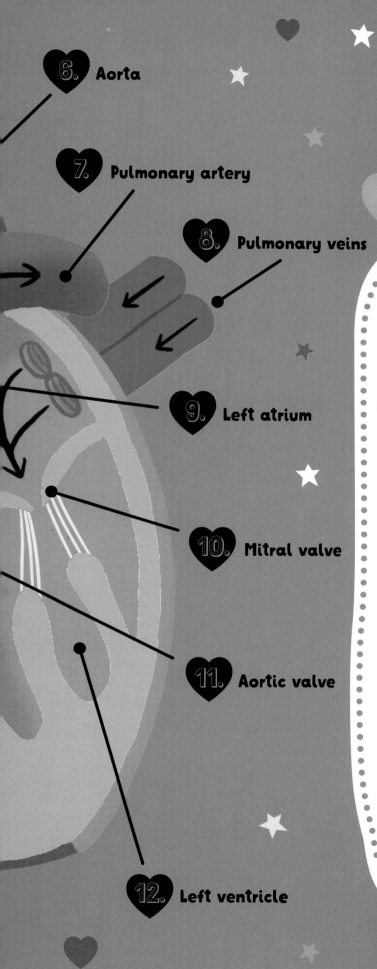

6. Aorta

7. Pulmonary artery

8. Pulmonary veins

9. Left atrium

10. Mitral valve

11. Aortic valve

12. Left ventricle

HOW the HEART Works in 5 Steps

The heart is an organ that works like a big pump to push oxygenated blood around your body through a network arteries and veins (the circulatory system). Here's how it works:

1. The right atrium receives oxygen-poor blood from the body from the superior and inferior vena cava veins.

2. It pumps the blood to the right ventricle through the tricuspid valve.

3. The right ventricle then pumps the blood through the pulmonary valve into the pulmonary arteries. From here it is carried to the lungs to pick up oxygen once again.

4. The left atrium receives oxygen-rich blood from the lungs through the pulmonary veins and pumps it to the left ventricle through the mitral valve.

5. The left ventricle pumps the oxygen-rich blood through the aortic valve into the aorta, which then carries it to the rest of the body, full of the oxygen and nutrients it needs.

3 Party Tricks NOT Everyone Can Do

1.
Wiggling ear:
an ear wiggle is created by twitching the muscles just above the ears. Studies suggest that it's genetic, so if you don't have the wiggling gene, you'll never master it.

2.
Bending thumbs backward:
being able to bend your thumb backward is due to hypermobility, which means joints can stretch farther than normal. It's known as being double-jointed, although there aren't really two joints, just one mega flexible one.

3.
The Vulcan salute:
invented by the actor who played the character of Mr. Spock in Star Trek, this hand gesture involves raising your palm and separating your little finger and ring finger from your middle and index fingers, and also separating the thumb. No one's certain whether it has anything to do with genetics, but some find it easy while others struggle. **Keep trying!**

3 TONGUE TRICKS

1. ROLLING YOUR TONGUE
Studies show that around 70 percent of people have the tongue-rolling gene and can roll their tongues into a tube.

2. TONGUE TO NOSE
Only 10 percent of people have a tongue long enough to touch their nose.

3. CLOVERLEAF TONGUE
This is the rarest of the tricks: the tongue is compressed in two places, making it look as though it has three sections. It's also known as trefoil tongue.

7 ICKY BODY FLUIDS

1. Plasma

White-yellow liquid containing water, proteins, salts, and white blood cells. Plasma is mixed with our red blood cells and makes up over half of our blood. Its functions include fighting infections, clotting blood, and forming scabs.

2. Blood

A mixture of white and red blood cells, water and tiny cells called platelets (which help to clot blood). It's responsible for delivering oxygen around the body and removing waste.

3. Urine

Liquid waste made by the kidneys to carry toxins out of the body. It is light yellow in color, and gets darker if you haven't drunk enough water.

4. Phlegm

A type of mucus, which is made in the lungs to capture any particles as air passes into the lungs. It's usually pale or clear, but you might cough up yellowy green phlegm when you have a cold or a chest infection.

5. Pus

A yellowish fluid that collects at the site of an infection. It contains dead bacteria and dead white blood cells that have finished fighting the infection.

6. Mucus

A thick stringy fluid produced in many areas of the body that protects and moisturizes the organs to stop them from drying out. It also traps bacteria and dirt.

7. Ear wax

Also known as cerumen, ear wax is made up of dead skin cells, hair, and oils. It protects the ears from bacteria, dirt, and water. It can be orange, wet and sticky, or dry and gray.

7 EXERCISES to RAISE YOUR HEART RATE

It's good for you to get your heart pumping faster every so often, because it strengthens the heart and trains your body to move blood and oxygen more efficiently.

1. Climbing stairs
Uses the big leg muscles, which need more oxygen.

2. Windmilling
Making circles with your arms in vertical wheels up and over your head.

3. Dancing
Fun as well as being great exercise.

4. Jumping jacks
Leaping up from a standing position and landing with legs and arms spread out, then leaping back to the center again.

5. Playing sports
Whether you like soccer, basketball, swimming, or cycling, playing sports regularly is a good way to raise your heart rate.

6. High knees
Jogging on the spot and raising the knees as high as you can.

7. Skipping
Jumping is great exercise. Skipping every day will improve your fitness.

4 USELESS Body BITS

Did you know we have some parts that do absolutely nothing important? Most of them are thought to be left over from hundreds of thousands of years ago in our evolutionary past.

1. Auricular muscles—our distant mammal relatives used these muscles to turn their ears to detect approaching danger, but they have little or no use now, unless you count ear wiggling.

2. Coccyx—a bumpy bit at the bottom of the spine, thought to be a leftover tailbone from our ancestors.

3. Palmaris longus— a muscle that runs from the inside wrist to the elbow, thought to be useful in a time when we climbed trees. Ten percent of people are born without it.

4. Pyramidalis muscle— serves no obvious purpose, though it can help with tensing the front of the stomach.

4 Examples of Mind OVER Matter

It's possible to control our bodies with our minds . . .

1. Some Tibetan monks and Indian yogis are able to suspend normal body functions during deep meditation, including slowing their heart rate to a near stop.

2. The "placebo effect" is when patients think they're taking real medicine, when in fact they're taking harmless pills containing no medicine. The effect is often positive, proving that patients can sometimes improve their health using the power of belief.

3. Psychologist Ellen Langer told half of a cleaning team that their work was burning lots of calories. That half of the team then lost weight, while the others stayed the same—all because of the power of the mind.

4. When Tom Boyle Jr. saw a car run over a child, he picked up the car so that the boy could be pulled free—even though the car weighed as much as a rhinoceros! He was able to summon so much strength because of adrenalin—the chemical produced by the body when we're angry, frightened, or excited—and pure determination!

4 POPULAR Alternative MEDICINES

These medicines might be different from the kind you're used to.

1. Ayurvedic medicine—comes from ancient Indian techniques of using plants and minerals, along with massage, to help drain toxins from the body.

2. Reflexology—concentrates on pressure points in the hands, feet, and face to reach other parts of the body connected to them by the nervous system.

3. Acupuncture—inserting very thin needles into different points in the body, believed to stimulate nerves and release pain-relieving chemicals.

4. Hypnotherapy—after placing you in a deep state of relaxation, hypnotherapists try to help you change your behavior or mood by dealing with thoughts that are deep in the subconscious.

5
SWEAT TRIGGERS

1. Hot weather—sweat cools the skin as it evaporates, taking some of our body heat with it.

2. During a fever—raising our temperature is one of the body's ways of fighting off an infection.

3. Exercise—when we exercise our heart rate quickens as our muscles work harder, causing a rise in temperature. This triggers the sweat glands to help us cool down.

4. Spicy food—chilis can make you sweat because a chemical in them called capsaicin excites the nerves that respond to heat, making us think we need to cool down.

5. Scary stuff—being scared releases adrenalin, a chemical that floods through us to help us run faster. It speeds up the heart, which triggers sweating.

6
SWEATY FACTS

1. Watery salty sweat is made in the eccrine glands and comes out through your skin pores. There are 2 million of them all over your body.

2. Oily, thick sweat comes from apocrine glands, located in the armpits and groin area. These glands don't have their own pores but use hair follicles to send sweat to the surface.

3. Apocrine glands only start working when you reach puberty.

4. Armpit sweat contains pheromones: silently stinky hormones. You can't consciously smell them but your body does detect and react to them.

5. Smelly sweat—or body odor (BO)—occurs when the bacteria living on our skin feed on sweat and break it down into stinky chemicals.

6. Keeping clean and using a deodorant can help keep smells at bay. And it's best to air shoes and wear fresh socks every day, because our feet can produce a lot of sweat, which feeds a lot of bacteria.

6 ALPHABETIC
Vitamins

Vitamins are molecules that nourish your body and keep it healthy. We get most of them from a varied diet.

1. Vitamin A—helps the immune system function.
Sources: cheese, milk, eggs, oily fish

2. The B Vitamins: B1 (Thiamine), B2 (Riboflavin) and B3 (Niacin), Pantothenic Acid, B6, B7 (Biotin), Folic acid, B12—help form blood cells and aid the nervous system, eyes, and skin.
Sources: fruit, eggs, meat, fish, grains, and vegetables

3. Vitamin C—good for cells, blood vessels and recovery from illness. Sources: fruit, especially citrus, and vegetables

4. Vitamin D—good for muscles, bones, and teeth.
Sources: red meat and oily fish, egg yolks and sunlight!

5. Vitamin E—helps the immune system to keep eyes and skin healthy.
Sources: nuts, seeds, plant oils, wheatgerm

6. Vitamin K—aids blood clotting to heal wounds.
Sources: leafy greens, vegetable oils, and cereal grains

4 UNWELCOME
VISITORS

If you're not squeamish, take a look at these parasites— unwelcome visitors to the human body.

1. Bed bugs
Little dark-red bugs that can hide in bedrooms and drink our blood while we sleep, causing rashes and itching.

2. Head lice
Lice that lay their eggs (nits) in our hair and drink our blood, causing intense itching. They spread when heads touch together, which is why they spread fast through schools.

3. Scabies mites
These teeny tiny mites lay their eggs under our skin and are horribly itchy. They spread through human contact.

4. Demodex mites
Weeny mites that live in our eyelashes and eyebrows. Under a microscope they look a little bit like crocodiles. They eat the oils from hair follicles, but generally go unnoticed and are harmless for most people.

3 TIPS *on* Muscle-building Food

Working out with weights makes muscles bigger and stronger, but to work out you need energy too. This is how serious body builders eat, but if they gave up weightlifting and continued to eat like this, they would become overweight very quickly.

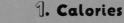

1. Calories
Eat more than your body burns. For example, bulk up on pasta, bread, dried fruits, and seeds.

2. Protein
Your body needs lots of protein, for example meat, fish, eggs, and nuts, to recover from workouts and help your muscles grow larger.

3. Regular meals
Eat lots of smaller meals throughout the day instead of just two or three big ones.

3 Things About *Pee*

Pee contains lots of information because it shows what your body has been trying to get rid of. Doctors can test it in a laboratory, but there are some things you can tell just by looking at it…

1. Healthy pee comes in a range of yellows, from watery pale to mustard-color. The lighter the color, the more hydrated you are. If pee is dark yellow you probably need to drink more water.

2. What we eat can change the color of pee. Beetroot turns it pink, while carrots can make it orange, and asparagus gives it a green tinge.

3. Some foods, such as asparagus, change the way your pee smells. Pee smells stronger if you're dehydrated or take vitamin supplements.

4 TYPES of Sugar

When you're looking at lists of ingredients on food packaging, you might not be able to spot the sugar. Here are some common types:

1. **Fructose**: found in fruits and honey.
2. **Glucose**: found in honey, fruits, and vegetables.
3. **Maltose**: found in barley.
4. **Sucrose**: made up of glucose and fructose and found in plants.

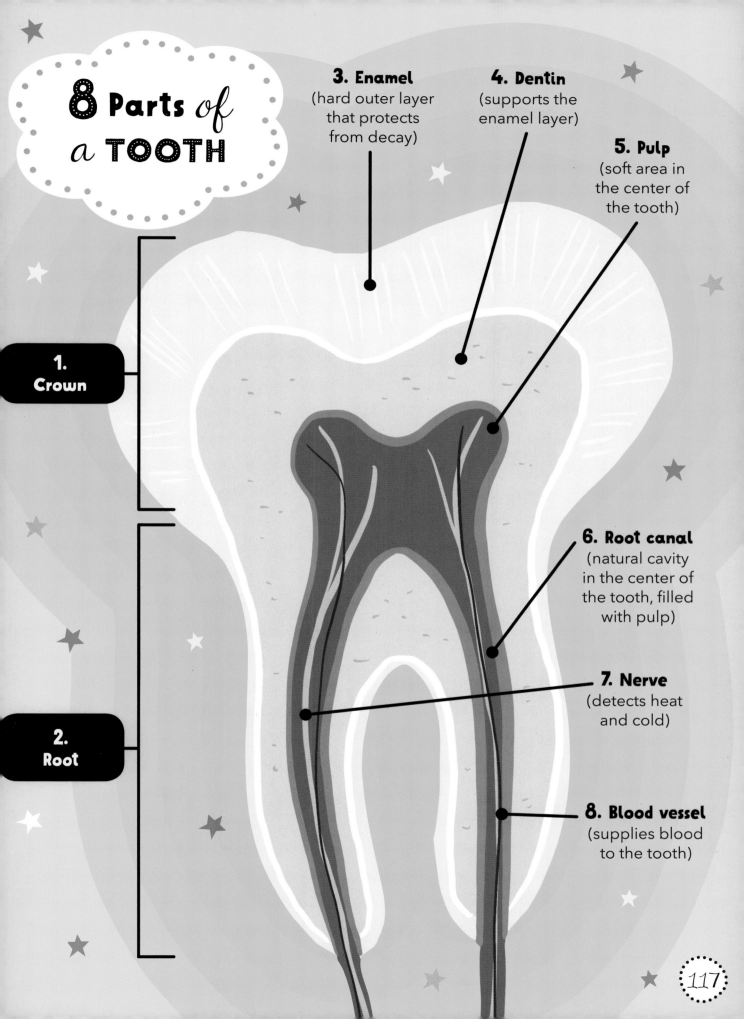

8 Parts of a TOOTH

3. Enamel (hard outer layer that protects from decay)

4. Dentin (supports the enamel layer)

5. Pulp (soft area in the center of the tooth)

1. Crown

6. Root canal (natural cavity in the center of the tooth, filled with pulp)

7. Nerve (detects heat and cold)

2. Root

8. Blood vessel (supplies blood to the tooth)

10 Facts to Sneeze at

1. A sneeze can travel at up to 9 mph (14.5 km/h).

2. It can spray mucus up to 30 feet (9 m) away!

3. A sneeze gets rid of the dirt particles trapped by our nasal hairs.

4. Sneezes often come in twos or threes.

5. Some scientists believe we sometimes sneeze just to re-boot our nose functions.

6. Photic sneeze reflex is sneezing caused by looking at bright light—the brain may be confusing signals as the pupils contract in response to the light.

7. It is impossible to sneeze with your eyes open.

8. You can hold the urge to sneeze by rubbing your nose, or breathing out heavily through your nose.

9. A sneeze that's started shouldn't be stopped. Better out than in.

10. Sneezing doesn't happen in your sleep because the nerves that trigger sneezing are also sleeping.

7 SIGNS of Flu

Flu is a virus that makes you feel pretty rotten for a couple of weeks. It's like a bad cold but affects more than your nose. These are the tell-tale signs.

1. High fever—either feeling hot or having chills

2. **Muscle or body aches**

3. Coughing

4. **A sore throat**

5. Runny or stuffy nose

6. **Headaches**

7. Fatigue—feeling tired at times you wouldn't normally

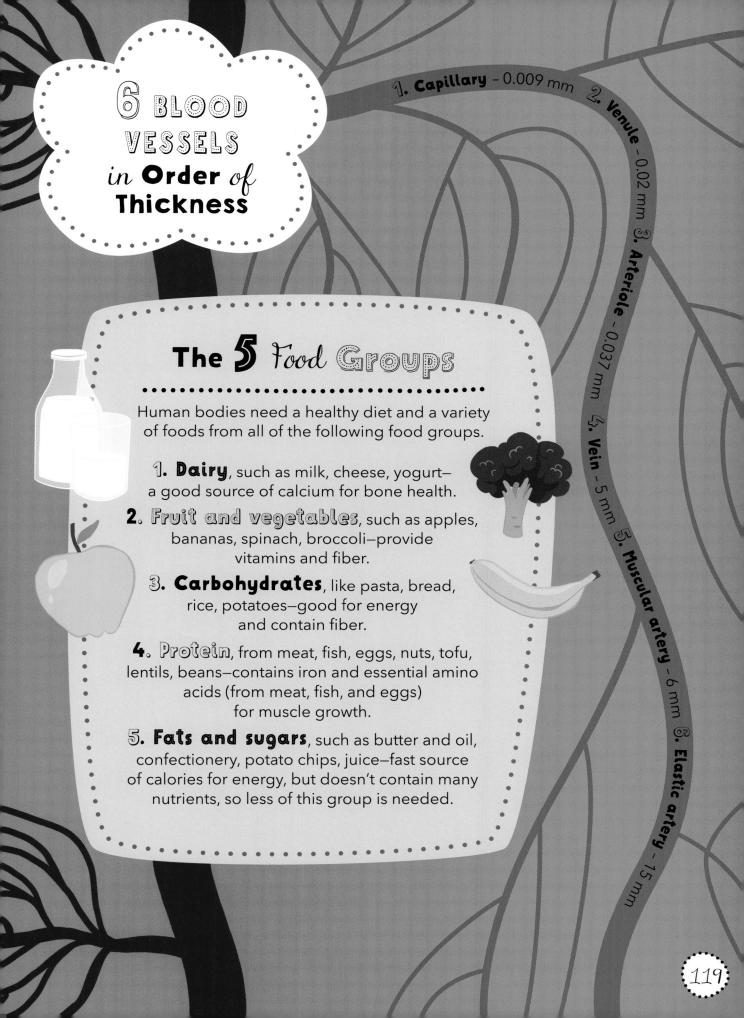

6 BLOOD VESSELS in **Order** of **Thickness**

1. **Capillary** - 0.009 mm   2. **Venule** - 0.02 mm   3. **Arteriole** - 0.037 mm   4. **Vein** - 5 mm   5. **Muscular artery** - 6 mm   6. **Elastic artery** - 15 mm

The **5** Food Groups

Human bodies need a healthy diet and a variety of foods from all of the following food groups.

1. **Dairy**, such as milk, cheese, yogurt—a good source of calcium for bone health.

2. **Fruit and vegetables**, such as apples, bananas, spinach, broccoli—provide vitamins and fiber.

3. **Carbohydrates**, like pasta, bread, rice, potatoes—good for energy and contain fiber.

4. **Protein**, from meat, fish, eggs, nuts, tofu, lentils, beans—contains iron and essential amino acids (from meat, fish, and eggs) for muscle growth.

5. **Fats and sugars**, such as butter and oil, confectionery, potato chips, juice—fast source of calories for energy, but doesn't contain many nutrients, so less of this group is needed.

119

11 Human Body Systems

The body has several systems—a set of body parts working together. They ensure that we live and function properly.

1. Skeletal system—bones, ligaments, tendons
Protects our organs and helps us move.

2. Nervous system—brain, spinal cord, nerves
Controls most of what the body does—walking, breathing, speaking, etc.

3. Lymphatic system—lymph nodes, lymphatic ducts, tonsils, and spleen and thymus gland
Makes and moves white blood cells around the body.

4. Immune system—tissues, cells, and chemicals throughout the body
Works with the lymphatic system to defend and protect the body against disease.

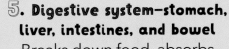

5. Digestive system—stomach, liver, intestines, and bowel
Breaks down food, absorbs nutrients, and disposes of waste.

6. Endocrine system—pituitary gland and thyroid
Produces hormones that affect growth, mood, and reproduction.

7. Circulatory system—heart, arteries, and veins
Moves blood around the body to deliver oxygen and nutrients.

8. Respiratory system—lungs, throat, nose, mouth
Responsible for breathing and oxygenating the blood.

9. Urinary system—kidney, bladder, urethra
Eliminates waste from the body and controls salt and mineral levels.

10. Muscular system—all the muscles of the body
Moves the body, supports and strengthens the skeletal system, and helps to pump blood.

11. Integumentary system—the skin, hair, and nails
Forms a barrier to protect the body from chemicals, UV rays, and disease.

6 Medical Patron SAINTS

1. Saint Luke the Evangelist, patron saint of doctors

2. Saint Blaise, patron saint of throat problems

3. Saint Rasso, patron saint of stomach pains, especially in children

4. Saint Agatha of Sicily, patron saint of nurses

5. Saint Cyriacus, patron saint of eye disease

6. Saint Apollonia, patron saint of dentists

7 Poop SHAPES

Want to know what your poop says about you? The Bristol Stool scale is a chart that doctors use to check if your poop is healthy, or perhaps a sign that something stinks.

1. Type 1—hard little pellets—difficult to pass (constipation)
You may not be drinking enough water and eating enough fiber.

2. Type 2—hard lumpy sausage shape—a bit of a strain to pass
Dehydrated. Drink more plain water.

3. Type 3—like a dry sausage, cracked—fairly easy to pass
This is a healthy poop.

4. Type 4—smooth sausage—easy to pass
This is also a healthy poop.

5. Type 5—soft blobs that hold together—easy to pass
Perhaps you ate something different or are feeling stressed.

6. Type 6—fluffy mushy blobs with no shape—very easy to pass (diarrhea)
You could have a vitamin deficiency, a reaction to medication, or a food intolerance.

7. Type 7—liquid (diarrhea)
This could be a sign that you aren't well, perhaps due to a virus or infection, and you should see a doctor.

7 FALSE TEETH from the Ghastly PAST

Today's false teeth are made from plastic, which hasn't always been available for people with missing teeth ...

1. Animal teeth—cattle and horse teeth were popular choices.

2. Ivory (the tusks of hippos, walruses, and elephants) was made into dentures. Ivory teeth became stained and smelly after a while.

3. Bone—used to make false teeth from Ancient Roman times.

4. Porcelain—the same material used to make cups and sinks—was used from the 18th century, but it was easily chipped.

5. Gold—if you were rich enough and wanted to show it every time you smiled, you might have a gold set of dentures. Single gold teeth are sometimes used to replace missing or damaged teeth today.

6. Wood—wooden false teeth were popular from the Middle Ages, but more common in China and Japan than in Europe.

7. Human teeth—horrible but true, human teeth were used as dentures. They might be pulled from executed criminals, or from dead people on battlefields.

4 ODDLY Named Body PARTS

1. Zonule of Zinn, found in the eye
2. Space of Disse, found in the liver
3. Island of Reil, found in the brain
4. Bachmann's bundle, found in the heart

6 Ways to KEEP Your Brain Brainy

Keep your brain fit with these top brain-training tips.

1. **Do puzzles**—crosswords, logic puzzles, and math puzzles like sudoku.

2. **Read**—excellent for memory and learning skills. When you're really involved in a good story, your brain can't tell the difference between reading and actually experiencing it!

3. **Use your hands**—experiment with painting, drawing, music, or other arts and crafts.

4. **Physical exercise**—exercise helps to bring oxygen-rich blood to the brain, increasing its efficiency and making you feel good.

5. **Improve your diet**—healthy food helps your mind as well as your body.

6. **Be sociable**—spend time with your friends (preferably face-to-face!).

9 Big In-a-Lifetime NUMBERS

These numbers are based on an average person living to 80 years old.

1. **672,768,000** breaths
2. **229,961** hours of sleep
3. **216,262,500** steps
4. **3,363,840,000** heartbeats
5. **840,960,000** blinks
6. **7,506 gallons (28,413 liters)** of saliva
7. **1 quadrillion** (1 million billion) bits of information held in the brain
8. **420,480,000,000** dead skin cells
9. **109,983 miles (177,000 km)** of walking

24 Human Body Words and Their Meanings

1. **Anatomy**—study of the structure of the body of a living thing.

2. **Antibody**—a substance that kills germs.

3. **Artery**—blood vessel that carries blood away from the heart.

4. **Cartilage**—flexible but tough tissue, like bendy bone.

5. **Cell**—tiny building blocks of living things, which contain a nucleus with genetic material.

6. **Germ**—a microscopic organism that spreads disease, such as bacteria and viruses.

7. **Hormone**—messenger molecules that carry information to organs.

8. **Host**—the living body on which a parasite lives and feeds (see parasite).

9. **Ligament**—tough, stretchy tissue that connects bones in a joint.

10. **Membrane**—thin sheet of cells or tissue acting as a lining or divider.

11. **Mental**—relating to the mind.

12. **Microorganism**—a life form so small you need a microscope to see it.

13. **Molecule**—the smallest unit of a substance.

14. **Muscle**—soft tissue that moves the body by pushing and pulling.

15. **Neuron**—a cell within the nervous system that passes on messages.

16. **Neurotransmitter**—chemical molecule carrying a message, passed between neurons and muscles, for example.

17. **Nutrient**—a source of food or fuel for the body.

18. **Organ**—a part of the body that has a very specific function.

19. **Organ transplant**—taking a part of one body and placing it in another body.

20. **Parasite**—a creature that lives in or on another animal, often causing irritation or illness.

21. **Physical**—relating to the body.

22. **Surgery**—treating an illness or injury with an operation.

23. **Tendon**—strong tissue connecting muscle to bone.

24. **Vein**—a tube in the body which carries blood back to the heart.

INDEX

Page numbers in **bold** indicate a complete list.

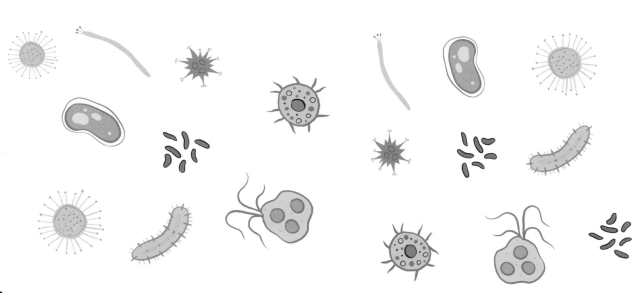